What's a Nice God Like You Doing in a Place Like This?

A Completely Unorthodox Devotional Guide

Jim Dant

&

Becky Ramsey

© 2016

Published in the United States by Faithlab, Macon GA.
www.faithlab.com

ISBN # 978-0-9895753-3-1

For the incredibly gifted staff of
First Baptist Church, Greenville, South Carolina,
who constantly remind us not to take ourselves too seriously.

Contents

Introduction

Life is messier than most devotional guides suggest. Many devotional writers seem to dwell daily in the land of ocean waves, wispy clouds, cute children, and flowers. Their experiences reflect the dreams of Katie—the lovable character from the movie *Horton Hears a Who*—who exclaims, "In my world everyone is a pony, and they all eat rainbows and poop butterflies." Our lives are messier than that. We're guessing yours is too.

So this devotional guide is filled with snakes and album covers and cat urine and underwear and porn stars and screaming kids and, well, you get the picture—all those messy places in life that seem completely void of the presence of anything holy yet provide us with a glimpse of God's holiness. Rather than smiling and dismissing the moments, we decided to journal a few thoughts about God's presence amid all this messiness. We asked the obvious question—"What's a nice God like you doing in a place like this?"—and it ended up being the perfect pickup line, because God walked with us to the next messy moment.

Having quoted Dr. Seuss, it would only be balanced to quote Shakespeare as well. In *A Midsummer Night's Dream*, Puck's closing monologue begins,

> If we shadows have offended,
> Think but this and all is mended,
> That you have but slumber'd here
> While these visions did appear.
> And this weak and idle theme,
> No more yielding but a dream,
> Gentles, do not reprehend:
> If you pardon, we will mend. (V.i.1–8)

Okay, we probably won't mend anything, but we would like you to pardon us. We're only human. We know you are too. And God loves hanging out with us humans. Read on…

1

Spotting God...

While Wearing a Paper Gown

"You'll need to undress down to your panties," says the nurse, handing me the paper gown. "It opens in the back. And any makeup you're wearing will have to come off. She's got you scheduled for a full body scan, so she needs to see your bare face. There's soap and gauze by the sink. Here's an extra paper sheet for your legs, just to keep you comfortable." Somehow I don't think the paper sheet is going to do it for me, but I take it and thank her.

This is how I pay for the sunburns of my life. Maybe you too? Fair-skinned people should not spend their teenage years marinating themselves in baby oil and sunbathing on aluminum foil blankets. This may sound obvious to you, but would somebody please travel back to 1980 and show me the paper gown?

I wipe off the makeup, strip to my undies, unfold the gown and put it on, then climb up onto the examining table. There's a mirror on the wall, and I see my crow's feet. I make a smile at myself, just to see how I look, and wish my face didn't have to be naked too. I look at my feet, pointing my toes in the mirror like a naked ballerina. My toenail polish is chipped. I should have redone it.

I sit on the table, waiting for my dermatologist to get things rolling, to walk in with her skinny self, her blonde hair, her pointy-toed shoes. I sit in my nakedness and wait.

The doctor comes in, and the nurse follows. She puts on gloves and starts to work, pulling up one arm from my side and running her eyes over it as if she's part machine, Locutus of Borg, scanning my arm from shoulder to fingertips. "Hmm," she says, and I feel myself tense. She pulls down the scope attachment to her glasses, closing in on a freckle on my forearm. I relax as she moves on, pulling apart my fingers and examining them like Ben used to do whenever he was bored at church. She turns my arm and scans the pale underside.

She slips my arms out of the sleeves of my gown exactly the way I used to undress my dolls. She lays the paper aside, and I close my eyes and imagine half of my naked Raggedy Ann chest out for all to see, its embroidered I LOVE YOU candy heart exposed. She moves parts of me and prods and pokes, then walks around to the other side of the chair and starts the practice all over again.

Does this bore her, or is it kind of fun, treasure hunting for disease, for things to freeze or snip? She touches my knee as she scans it, and I explain about the blue scar, how I accidentally jabbed a pencil lead into my leg in third grade and isn't it funny that I've been carrying around the sliver all this time. "Uh huh," she says. "Nothing to worry about; it's graphite, not lead." I know that already, but I don't say so. I don't tell her that I'm just trying to make conversation here, to soothe the awkwardness of being naked, of being poked and prodded.

She guides me to turn over with her gloved hands, and my brain entertains me with a vision of her trying to grab me with a giant set of tongs, to flip me to the other side like a hamburger, well done.

As she examines every last square inch of me, the skin hidden by my underwear, the backs of my knees, the bottoms of my feet, I wonder how I compare with other women my age. Am I just another skin-wrapped body walking around to her, or does she find me odd in any way? Will she talk about me to her husband as they eat their salad and pass the bread? I know she has to do the looking—that it's the whole reason I came—but still I wonder: How do I measure up?

It's a human question.

I feel the lamp light on me and hear the scrawl of the pen on paper as she surveys my land formations, and I'm not scared, just uncomfortable. She gets out the spray can of liquid nitrogen and aims it at a couple of spots on my legs. This is nothing, I know, but I get squeamish easily, so I try to think of other things. I ask myself what God would say to me here in this room. Psalm 139 comes to mind:

I've searched you, and I know you, dear one. I know when you sit on an examining table and when you get up and put on your clothes. I hear your thoughts, and I hear your fears. I'm the one, you know, who knit you together in your mother's womb. I know where you're weak and where you're strong, and I couldn't love you more, even in your brokenness.

I'm so thankful for God's merciful eyes that see and love beneath the surface.

BR

Imagine God looking upon you, examining you all over, and whispering in your ear. What do you hear God saying to you?

Spotting God...

From My Exoskeleton

Because a host of folk knows I'm a member of the clergy (and because a minority of folk knows I'm a closet monk), I'm often asked, "How do you pray?"

Well, usually I enter my office in the quiet of the morning. But on this particular morning, for the second morning in a row, I had scarce opened the prayer book when I heard it. I had attempted (to no avail) to meditate beyond the distraction yesterday. But today, the insidious cricket-leg-friction (chirping) was driving me crazy. Deciding to get on this insect's level, I left the comfort of my throne and began to creep—on hands and knees—toward the noise.

Following his incessant and irritating cries for help, I finally found him. He was wedged tight against the bottom of a bookshelf in the shadow of Kittel's *Theological Dictionary of the New Testament*, volume 9. If it had fallen on him, it would have killed him. If he had tried to read it, he would never have understood it. However, the likelihood of that book coming off the shelf was slim; it hasn't moved in twelve years. (Don't get me wrong. I use the other volumes all the time. I've just never needed to do research on any words beginning with Phi–Omega. You people are so gullible.)

I reached down with forefinger and thumb and picked him up by a hind leg. The pressure probably seemed excruciating to him, but I meant him no harm. I placed him in the palm of my left hand and then covered him with my right to keep him from leaping back into the abyss of my study. He leapt within the hollow of my hand, pounding his exoskeleton against the flesh of my half-closed fist. He was obviously afraid but in no danger of harm. I walked through the door of my study, down the church hallway, backed into the lever of the exterior door, turned, and took him to the courtyard lawn. I knelt down, opened my hand, and let him hop away. He was back in the familiar warmth of his world. The crisis was over. A new day and a new chapter of life were about to begin. There was no way he could ever understand the manner of his deliverance, but he was safe and free.

And that's how I pray.

JD

How do the sounds around you remind you of your prayers?

Spotting God...

In a Clay Pot

Are you a perfectionist too? It's one of those faults that we don't mind sharing. "I admit it, I'm a perfectionist," I've said in job interviews, watching the interviewer scribble on his pad—probably things like "Ooh, yes!" or "Conscientious!" or "Will neglect her own needs to make the company look good!" I've always thought it's a humble brag, not really a weakness.

"Not so fast!" says the clay pot on my desk.

The art teacher showed us how to make it. She handed each child in my second-grade class a big lump of clay, and within minutes the classroom became a snake factory, twenty-two seven- and eight-year-olds rolling out snakes on the tables with the palms of our hands. "Now, take the snakes and coil them around and around," she said as she demonstrated, turning the snakes into a spiral solid circle to form the bottom of the pot, and then around and around, higher and higher to form the sides.

Unfortunately, my snakes wouldn't behave. They refused to stack, sliding off each other and acting all wobbly and uneven. And when I pinched them together with my thumb and pointer, just like the teacher showed us, they got way out of whack. Some places were thin, and others were thick and bulgy. My pot was a lopsided mess.

Twice, I got frustrated and squished the pile together and started all over again. Why couldn't I do it? Everyone else was doing just fine. What was wrong with me? People were finishing, and I was starting over. Then they started cleaning up! I'd never finish. My face got hot, and my eyes got teary. I had to do something, so I balled up my clay and hid it in my fist and told the teacher I needed to go to the bathroom (teachers don't usually say no if you look really uncomfortable and hop around a little).

Once inside, I locked the door, knelt on the floor, rolled out the clay on the linoleum, and traced a circle with the pencil in my pocket. There, that would make the bottom. A smooth rectangle would do for the sides. I could pinch it around the bottom to serve as the cylinder wall. Hey, it didn't look so bad! It stood up tall and straight. But did it look too good? On everybody else's pots I could still see the individual coils of snake. The pencil! That's it! I dragged it around the walls in faux coil lines. Perfect! It was perfect!

I gathered my composure, sneaked in my pot to the table with everyone else's finished work, and got in line to go to the playground.

I don't remember the teacher's face, but when I look at my pot today, I have to laugh at how glaringly obvious it must have been. Somehow, my second-grade self hadn't noticed how different mine looked, a perfect little cylinder with drawn-in pencil lines beside everyone else's wobbly, bulgy stacks of snakes.

Maybe the other kids noticed, and maybe they didn't, but I knew I couldn't get it right, and I *had* to get it right—at least I thought I did. I had to make it look like I knew what I was doing. I had to make it perfect, so I turned it into a completely different thing than it was supposed to be.

I keep my pot on my desk to remember that little girl I was, the one ashamed and so scared to fail, the child willing to hide in the bathroom and cheat to earn approval. Poor little self! I also keep my pot on my desk to remind me of God, who sat there with me on the linoleum floor and stays with me still, loving me even when I can't love myself.

God calls me to let go of my perfectionism because it's mean to the girl God created. It keeps me from finishing things and starting new things and being the whole person of peace God made me to be.

No, perfectionism, I won't follow you. I'm sticking with God, who loves me for myself, with all my lopsided faults. Too bad if my snakes are bulgy or the paragraph I've rewritten nineteen times still doesn't feel exactly right. I will go on and maybe come back to edit later if I feel like it.

Or maybe not. I might just head to the playground.

BR

What did you struggle with as a child? What does God have to say to the child inside of you?

Spotting God...

In the Extremes

"I am Alpha and Omega...the beginning and the end." It's one of the ways God defines God's self. It's a short list of the places we can find easy audience with God—beginnings and endings.

I would concur with God (which is always a good thing). God is easily glimpsed in beginnings and endings. Sunrises and sunsets—the beginnings and endings of a day—are mesmerizing moments, displaying the artistic presence of God. The birth of a child and the death of a loved one—the beginnings and endings of life—tug us toward spiritual affirmations and questions concerning the presence of God. Nativity and crucifixion, creation and apocalypse, baptism and resurrection, diagnosis and cure—well, you get the picture.

I spend most of my time, however, in between these extremes. It's all those other letters (and their accompanying perceived divine absence) with which I struggle. They are the ones dominating the daily grind of my life—beta to psi, bet to shin, B to Y. Bills and cholesterol and dogs and eczema (I don't really have eczema, but it's a cool "e" word) and flat tires and gas prices and home repairs and—well, you get the picture.

JD

Using the ABCs, what challenges are you facing in your life today, and where might you see God in those challenges?

Spotting God...

When Urine Trouble

One of our cats urinated in the side pocket of my gym bag. While I commend the accuracy of his aim, his choice of target may require a contract to be issued on his furry tail.

The timing of his discharge was insignificant compared to the timing of my discovery. The bag was packed and ready to go. I hastily picked it up and threw it in the back of the VW, as is my daily habit. Arriving at the gym, I grabbed the bag, stuffed it in a locker, and proceeded to push and punish my body for over an hour. I took a shower and then opened the bag to retrieve my clothes. BANG! An unseen acidic mushroom cloud rose from the vinyl-lined portable locker.

What's a guy to do? I got dressed. Trying to mask the odor that had penetrated my clothing, I dabbed on a bit of cologne (which I now realize smells a bit like cat urine).

Not wanting to break the stride of my day, I headed to the coffee shop to write—and here I am. Several patrons have hurriedly passed my table, glancing in my direction with squinted, wondering eyes. A few others have outright stared. I've conjured several verbal responses to their odious ogling (although I would never dare speak these aloud): remaining close to the truth, "It's the last bit of cologne from a bottle I bought back in the 70s"; to the guys, "Haven't you ever smelled someone with an incredibly overabundant supply of testosterone?"; and to this one cute female, "It's just pheromones."

In the church we are marked by baptism, and people should know it; they should just be able to tell. In life we are often marked in other ways. We're "cat people" at our house. And in God's creative construction of the feline framework, cat people get marked.

JD

In what ways have you been marked by your baptism?

Spotting God...
In a Tee Shirt

Apparently, some people don't like my husband's orange tee shirt. Todd bought it in Atlanta a few years ago when our church youth group took an afternoon off from their mission work and toured the King Center, learning more about the work of Martin Luther King, Jr. The logo on the front reads, "nonviolence or nonexistence."

Todd wore it to baseball practice with Sam and hadn't thought anything about it until a dad on the field noticed it and grunted loudly in disgust. "You better be glad we're not nonviolent in America," the man said, "or else our country wouldn't be where it is today."

"He said WHAT?" I asked Todd from the kitchen as he put his glove in the closet.

"Yeah, it kinda surprised me too," Todd said. "Then he muttered something about bravery and gratitude."

"BRAVERY AND GRATITUDE?" I said a little too loudly, storming into the bedroom with the butcher knife still in hand.

Sam stuck his head in. "What's wrong?"

"Nothing," Todd said. "Go get your shower."

"Did you say anything back? Like maybe YOU SPENT FOUR YEARS OF YOUR LIFE IN THE AIR FORCE and what service did he ever do?"

"Why is Mom mad?" Sam asked.

"She's not mad," Todd said, "Go on and get in the shower."

Then Ben came in and wanted help with a calculus problem, and they left me standing there, holding the knife, dripping chicken juice on my bare feet, steaming.

I could just imagine the scene. The guy read the shirt and smacked a label on Todd's forehead: liberal—maybe even communist or socialist. Who knows? Labels fly these days.

I gritted my teeth and flew into an argument with the man in my head. By the time Todd and I finally got a moment to return to our conversation, I had a whole list of things to whack this guy over the head with in my defense of nonviolence (yes, I see the irony). Why don't you ask what this shirt is about before you start fussing at my husband? Do you think he's making an antiwar stance? What if he was? Maybe someone who actually served might have something to say about that.

Ask about Todd's brother's service in both gulf wars, in Afghanistan, in Bosnia. Todd's dad's service in the army. My granddad's service that cost him his life in WWII. They were all willing and glad to serve. So was Todd. Violence is sometimes necessary, but service members know the price better than anybody else.

Maybe that's part of why Todd wears the shirt. Maybe that's why he's such a believer in the words of Martin Luther King, Jr. And how is it braver to use violence anyway? Does nonviolence not require at least as much bravery?

When Todd walked back in the room, I was still living our previous conversation. "So what did you say? Surely you said something!"

"Yes, I said something," he said. "You ought to put that knife away."

"Tell me what you said first."

"I just looked at him, and I said I got the shirt at the King Center down in Atlanta. I said, 'You ought to go down there and tour it. It's a great place to take your kids, and it's only a couple hours' drive.' I told him you can see King's grave and learn more about his life and ministry and what he gave to our country. Then the guy wandered off and didn't say anything else."

Todd left the room, and I sat down on the bed, trying to keep my mouth from falling open. There I'd been, waving my knife around, ready to fight while he practiced what the shirt preached. No slamming doors, no smacking labels on people's foreheads, no accusing the guy of meaning anything in particular. Just a nonviolent response, inviting the guy into his circle instead of standing in the middle of it, throwing barbs his way.

Clearly I need to work on my standard invitation to widen the circle. I'm thankful I have someone I love—and a God I love—to show me how.

BR

How are you at widening the circle? Is there someone you need to welcome in?

Spotting God...

In Tragedy

We ran our errands Saturday morning, and as we drove through our neighborhood, I realized that Todd had been on a business trip and didn't know the tragic events that happened in our corner of the world midday Friday. Just a mile and a half from our house, Officer Allen Jacobs spotted 17-year-old Deontea Mackey and pulled over to ask him about a gun Mackey had been trying to buy. When Mackey gave chase, Officer Jacobs ran after him until Mackey fatally shot him. A half mile away, practically in the backyard of my church, police closed in on Mackey. He called his mother and then turned the gun on himself.

"But why was the officer chasing him?" Todd asked.

"You don't think they shouldn't have chased him?" Was he serious? "Todd, the kid was in a gang, had at least one gun, and was trying to get another! He had already committed one robbery at gunpoint," I barked.

"I haven't heard the story, Beck," Todd said. "That's why I'm asking."

I knew where Todd had been going with this. I had wondered it too when I heard the first details of what had happened. Was this one of those stories yet again? A kid just trying to live a kid's life, taken by the first, hidden instincts of someone sworn to protect him? But I'd had time to hear more, and this time the story hardened me.

"You know what? I don't have one bit of pity for that kid. Officer Jacobs had two young boys and a daughter on the way. He went to work to do his job, and now he's dead."

We sat in silence in the car, and I listened to my own words: *I don't have one bit of pity.* Wow, did I say that?

But it was hard to feel pity when I learned more about Officer Allen Jacobs. He played basketball on Friday nights with young men at the community center, near the site where he was murdered. Some of my kids at church knew Officer Jacobs from his visits to their elementary schools. He had served in the military and was a model police officer in our community.

It was hard to feel pity for someone who caused such pain, who took away a father, a son, a husband, a friend.

As people of faith, what do we do with this?

In worship on Sunday, we were getting ready for Easter. After the children brought in the palms, we prayed, *"Merciful God, we confess that we have sinned against you. The lips that sing 'Hosanna!' are the same that shout 'Crucify!'"*

This made me shiver in my pew. I'm one to shout praise: *Hosanna!* And then I have no pity: *Crucify!*

Whatever you've done to the least of these, you've done to me.

Does the least of these include 17-year-old boys like Deontea? Deontea Mackey killed Officer Jacobs. This can't be softened away. It was a grievous crime and leaves a family and community broken into pieces. Deontea also killed himself, and he was our Sam's age. They went to the same high school until he dropped out a year ago. "I didn't know him, Mom," Sam said. But I wonder if I did, just a little, in a way.

My first year of teaching, we lived in Washington, DC, where I taught a chemistry class for kids who had failed all their science courses and needed a science class to graduate. Some of them were barely hanging on. They'd endured years of others not believing in them or assuming things about them that they had to work around. Many were alarmingly professional at measuring chemicals on a balance, and the police entered my classroom on at least two occasions. But I loved them. I could not define them completely by their worst moments. I had seen too many glimmers of brightness, of cleverness, of laughter, of tenderness. Whatever they had done or not done, they were teenagers with possibilities.

Deontea ended the possibilities of Officer Allen Jacobs and his family, and he also ended his own possibilities. He chose to drop out of high school. He joined a gang. He committed egregious crimes. He killed a man.

But as Easter comes closer, I keep hearing a hymn:

> Were the whole realm of nature mine,
> that were an offering far too small;
> love so amazing, so divine,
> demands my soul, my life, my all.

Love demands my soul, my life, my all.

Love so amazing demands that I love. Love so amazing demands that I see all others as human beings. Love demands that I grieve Deontea Mackey as a child of God, treasured and loved and held and wept over. I'm sure God weeps with Deontea's mother and with others who loved him.

You have stored my tears in your bottle and counted each of them. (Ps 56:8)

Sometimes it's hard to imagine a bottle big enough.

BR

**What tough thing in your life today does amazing,
divine love demand of you?**

Spotting God...

In a Diagnosis

The emergency room doctor at St. Mary's Medical Center in San Francisco perused my x-rays, throat culture, and other gathered data. She shook her head, stared at her notes, and said aloud, "You've got conjunctivitis, laryngitis, a viral throat and sinus infection, as well as pneumonia. You've got a lot going on." In my mind, that was an understatement. Beyond my vivid sense of illness, I had a lot going on in my life. I was completing a church-wide retreat for Nineteenth Avenue Baptist Church in San Francisco, my granddaughter was two weeks away from her first birthday party, I'm scheduled to teach a class for Columbia Seminary, and the weeks that follow are filled with meetings with the Cooperative Baptist Fellowship, Baptist World Alliance, and summer youth camp. All of that is in addition to the usual schedule of preaching, meeting, visiting, and moving around First Baptist Greenville (SC). Yeah, I've got a lot going on.

My family physician made room in his schedule to see me upon my return to Greenville. He surveyed the analysis and conclusions of his West Coast contemporaries. He glanced at prescribed antibiotics and nodded with approval. I interrupted his thought process and inquired, "When am I going to feel better and be able to go back to work?" He stared at me for a moment and then began his lecture: "Did you know that prior to the invention of antibiotics, numerous people suffered from pneumonia? And did you know that most people who contracted pneumonia did not die? Do you know why? They rested until they were well." He paused before he said, "You need to stop talking and stop moving."

I've been quiet and still for days. It's given me a lot of time to think and to remember the words the psalmist recorded for us: "Be still, and know that I am God." Sometimes the best way to get through the difficulties of life is to stop the expenditure of our own energy, be quiet, be still, and let God do God's good work.

JD

Where do you need to make room for silence and stillness in your life?

Spotting God...
While Stoned

I had a kidney stone extracted last week. I was told weeks ago it was too large to leave my kidney. With it resting in my kidney, I could undergo lithotripsy—the painless sonic blasting of the stone—and the resulting pieces would be evacuated with ease. But…it left my kidney. After a painful two-day trek down my left side, it lodged about two inches from my bladder in the natural curve of my ureter. (Was that graphic enough for you? It gets worse.) In this position, lithotripsy was no longer an option. It had to be extracted.

The urologist's preoperative consult was sobering. He was planning to go spelunking in my privates. He told me he was going to take a camera, flashlight, laser gun, and basket into "mammoth cave" (what did you expect me to call it?). He intended to locate the stone, blast it into pieces, collect the pieces in his basket, and pull them out. He did.

Three hours later, I opened my eyes, blinked, and struggled to focus on the nurse who was supervising my immediate recovery. Every part of my body felt sore—some parts more than others. She informed me I had a stent in my ureter. It ran from my bladder to my kidney and was intended to keep the irritated passageway open so my body could rid itself of toxic waste during the healing process. My semi-sedated mind began to wander: *Stent… Lent…stent…Lent. They rhyme. Wow. Anesthesia is amazing. And Lent is like a stent because it intentionally opens a prayerful passage between my heart and heaven so the toxic tendencies of my life can be dealt with during these days of healing prior to Easter, and then…*

Then the doctor touched my shoulder. Interrupting the meandering meditations of my mind, he informed me the stent would be removed in three days. *Did he say "three days"? Like the stent in my ureter, Jesus was in the grave for three days, and then on Easter morning…* Touching my shoulder again, he asked if I was paying attention. He further explained that after three days, he would go back into "mammoth cave" and pull the stent out with a pair of pliers (at least that's what I think he said). I am certain about his last comment, however: "You will not be anesthetized for the removal procedure." He assured me the pain would be brief and that everything would be in perfect working order after the stent was removed.

For now, I am healing, evacuating, and waiting. That's what we do with stents—and with Lent—until the third day.

JD

What painful moment in your life could be compared to the rigors of the Lenten season?

Spotting God...

Behind the
Green Door

The day after Easter 2009 was fateful for some of our fellow earthlings. Joe Cabuk (whose name most folk will not recognize) died in an airplane. The airplane didn't crash, however. Joe was the pilot. He died in the cockpit—while in flight! Fortunately, a passenger on board the twin-engine plane had flight experience and was able to safely land the aircraft. One of Joe's friends commented, "Joe died in the seat of an airplane. It's where he loved to be."

On this same Monday, Harry Kalas died. Sports fans knew Harry as the long-time voice of the Philadelphia Phillies. He had spent decades calling the plays via radio and television for last year's Major League World Champions. He was found dead Monday in the Philadelphia broadcast booth. One of Harry's colleagues reportedly remarked, "He died in the broadcast booth. It's where he loved to be."

This morning, I learned that Marilyn Chambers also died Monday. Marilyn was a 1970s porn star with leading roles in the movies *Behind the Green Door, Insatiable,* and many others (so I'm told). She was discovered while working for Ivory Snow detergent (you can't make this stuff up). She was found dead in her bed this past Monday. None of her friends or colleagues has reportedly said "She died in the bed. It's where she loved to be," but everyone was thinking it.

All tongue-in-cheek humor aside, my prayers went out to each of these families today. Loss is loss. Grief is grief. I was intrigued, however, that each died living life. They died in the places that defined them.

Living well and dying well are two great goals of our existence. I'm going to keep driving my convertible on Saturdays; preaching on Sundays; strumming the guitar, reading, writing, attending concerts, playing poker, piddling with Hebrew, and hugging my kids when I get the chance. And if I die doing any of those things, I will have lived and died well. But I hope I don't have to look behind the green door (or the pearly gate or whatever) until many more Easters and many more Mondays have passed.

JD

Where do you experience joy in your life? Where do you live, and what would you like to be doing when you die?

Spotting God...

At the Alteration Shop

One Wednesday morning, Todd went to see Sheila at her alterations shop. I've changed Sheila's name, but she's a real person, a woman with steel-strong hands from years of wrestling difficult zippers and forcing sharp needles through tough upholstery fabrics.

Sheila's the lady Todd goes to whenever he needs his trousers hemmed or a jacket taken in or has other mending needs that his sewing-proficient partner in life could do if she (a) found the projects more interesting or (b) wasn't frightened of knits.

When Todd brought her his ripped cycling pants, she was watching the news as she worked, shaking her head about a recent terrorist attack overseas. "It's the Muslims again," she said, taking his pants in hand. "Kill, kill, kill, kill. It's what they do. It's in their Quran, you know."

Sheila is a Christian and freely talks about it. "But Sheila," Todd said, "most Muslims are peaceful. I have friends who are Muslim. They're not like that."

"Sorry, but they're exactly like that," Sheila said. "They're just hiding it. Look; I'll show you." She pulled a Quran from a stack of books behind a sewing machine. "See that yellow?" she said, flipping pages to show the highlighting. "That's all the killing verses."

"But don't you think we could do the same thing with our Old Testament?" Todd said. "There's plenty of killing and destruction there. But it's not the central message, is it?"

"Well, there's only one solution as I see it, and that's that we get rid of them before they get rid of us." She looked up at the television and nodded at the news coverage of the upcoming election. "We need a leader who understands power. That's what we need. Power and somebody who isn't pussyfooting around, trying to sound politically correct all the time. We need Jesus, and we need power. Put them together and we have a chance at surviving."

It's clear that Todd's cycling pants weren't the only thing she was trying to alter.

I realize, of course, that terrorism isn't something we can love away, that it takes not only careful thought but serious action. But after our Good Friday service at church, I can't help but bristle (or get physically sick) at Sheila's coupling of Jesus Christ with a hunger for power. At our service we heard the stories of Jesus praying in the garden, of Judas betraying him, of Peter disowning him, of the guards mocking him, of the crown of thorns and the cross, of Jesus telling Peter to put the sword away. We were invited, if we felt led, to go forward and place our hands or heads on a cross that had been set prone on the floor of our chapel, to pray prayers of confession or thanksgiving.

I could not do it. I prayed from my pew. After a week of swirling and brewing with more emotion than I could handle, I knew that if I laid my forehead on that cross, I would not be able to hold it in. I had been altered, but not by power.

By the all-powerful love of God, expressed in the meekness and humility of people I dearly loved and people I had never met.

By a mother and father who so loved their new son that they dared to ask us to walk beside them in an uncertain journey.

By a father weeping in my office because he could identify with a child in pain in our congregation.

By a two-year-old smoothing lotion on the feet of her grandmother as she struggles with cancer, saying, "I want to help; I want to help."

By a parent refusing his pain medication after a recent surgery so he could attend a meeting to show support for a family he loved.

By a friend who recently lost the love of her life yet is bravely trying to trust God that she will survive the loss and is letting others know that she needs help.

I'm so thankful for these people in my life, for the way they wrestle with and mend my corner of the world. The fabric is tough and the needles sharp, but I see them work the way Jesus did: prayerfully, courageously, selflessly. May we all live into that kind of love!

BR

Who has altered you in recent days, showing you God's love and mercy?

Spotting God...

In Vinyl

Yesterday, the children of our church processed, waved palms, and sang. It was a vivid, annual signal that Holy Week had arrived.

In the early hours of this morning (Monday), I topped off my coffee and tiptoed down the stairs into my basement. I flicked on the fluorescents and scoured the shelves of music. This cavern beneath our home is a private Hard Rock Café. Autographed guitars, drumheads, posters, and concert tickets adorn the building-block walls. Each evokes a memory of time spent in close proximity to Pink, Carole King, Jason Mraz, Alice Cooper, Kate Campbell, Kenny Wayne Shepherd, the Atlanta Rhythm Section, Widespread Panic, Avril Lavigne, Peter Frampton, and a host of others. Beneath these cherished icons are shelves of music—a forty-seven-year lifetime of CDs, cassettes, 8-tracks, and vinyls. All are separated by genre and alphabetically stored by artist.

During Holy Week, I typically make my way to the classical CDs and spend a portion of each morning pondering the vocalizations of a popular requiem. In years past I've overused Rutter's (my personal favorite) but have also had my soul lifted by the compositions of Fauré, Mozart, Brahms, and Dvorak. Today, however, my gaze traveled past these treasured pieces and lay fixed on a vinyl title.

I like vinyl. I've heard arguments about the digital accuracy of CDs and the faulty friction between needles and grooves, but I still like vinyl. I can't scientifically explain it, but vinyl is warm. It crackles like a fire and hypnotically spins and smells like days past—characteristics that can't be digitally captured. Of all the vinyls I own, I cherish none more than *Frampton Comes Alive!* This morning, my gaze fixed on that vinyl title. It seemed to scream at me, "Play me! I'm an Easter album! *Frampton Comes Alive!*" I followed the Spirit and gently placed the dark halo on my turntable. Before the morning had ended, I had listened to both sides of both albums—a true Holy Week experience. How could you miss with titles like "Something's Happening," "Show Me the Way," "It's a Plain Shame," "All I Want to Be Is by Your Side," "Shine On," and "Do You Feel Like We Do?"? And even the ever-popular cover tune—"Jumpin' Jack Flash"—offered these words: *I was drowned; I was washed up and left for dead. I fell down to my feet, and I saw they bled. I frowned at the crumbs of a crust of bread. I was crowned with a spike right thru my head. But it's all right now.* Add to all that—the guy's name is Peter!

In a couple hours I was inundated with Easter metaphor and had enjoyed the rush of a hundred resurrected memories from my early high school days. I was also late to work…

JD

What "secular" albums or songs have spoken volumes to your faith?

Spotting God...

In an Aversion to Nails

I love the word *Eastertide*. It sounds like Easter break at the beach—when you're still full of jellybeans and Peeps, still reveling in the mystery and beauty and triumph of Easter, still humming "Lift High the Cross" and "Up from the Grave He Arose," and the stories just keep washing over you as you walk barefoot in the sun. The stories swirl around your feet as the sand pulls away, crashing at your knees sometimes—and when you're not paying attention, they soak you right through the skin and into your heart as well, matching their beat to yours: Love won, love won, love won.

On the children's hall we relish our Eastertide stories—the tales of what happened *after* the resurrection; the surprise appearances of a Jesus who would not leave his people until they were ready.

One recent Sunday, our teachers shared the story of the women finding the empty tomb. Lucky for me, after the story was told, they wrote down the children's responses to the questions they asked: "Are there any parts of this story we could leave out and still have all the story we need?" I love this question because it makes the children measure out each ingredient of the story, hold it in their hands, weigh it, examine it, and search it for value. One child said, "Did we really need the boulder since it was rolled away anyway?" to which another child said, "Yes, we do, because people would think Jesus's body could have been taken and it was all a trick." But one second-grader said something I can't get out of my mind: "Did they really have to use nails on the cross? Couldn't we leave them out? Couldn't they put him on the cross another way?"

Oh, child, I hear what you're saying.

When I was 17, our youth group held a backyard Bible club at a campground as part of a summer mission trip. One of the young men on our team decided that if we really wanted to bring kids to Christ, we needed to get right to the point of things and focus on the crucifixion. The industrious teenage evangelist brought with him a box of nails to hand out to all the children as a gruesome party favor/visual aid. "Put the nail on your palm," he told the happy campers. "Feel the point; push it in a little. Now imagine someone using a hammer to drive it through your hand. Imagine the steel tearing through your flesh. Imagine the blood and the broken bones and the pain. Jesus did that for you to save you from your sins. Making him your savior is the least you can do."

I'd never want to soft pedal the story of the crucifixion, of the agony and torture Jesus faced. I tell the story to elementary-aged children, and I don't leave anything out. But I also know the danger of using guilt and emotional manipulation with children to drive them to Jesus because they "owe him their souls." Faith based on guilt and fear will not stand. It is not healthy. It is abusive. Of course we owe God everything, as every good thing comes from God. But I want children to fall in love with Jesus the Christ because of who he was and is, not because they feel beholden. What kind of love would that be?

The kids and I love how Pastor Jim explains it. The world did its very worst to Jesus, and God responded by giving us God's best, a risen savior who reaches out to everyone still, even those who worked to destroy him. That's the kind of Christ and the kind of God I want children to know.

So what do we tell the child who wishes there hadn't been nails? The child who wishes he could have been killed in a kinder, gentler way? I'd give him a hug and say I agree. I'd say that I wish it hadn't happened at all, but because it did, God turned it into a most precious, amazing gift. No matter what horrors people face on earth—and goodness knows our world is full of horrors—we know our God has borne it. God knows how it feels, how nauseating it is, how soul- and body-crushing, how exhausting and breath-stealing and awful. And God weeps with us, or maybe in place of us, when we've become hardened and can't feel it anymore.

The stories wash over us. Yes, there were nails—on the cross, in his body—but God doesn't want us to roll around in the agony, celebrating the pain. God wants us to celebrate the empty tomb, the risen Jesus who is ours forever, the hands that reach out to welcome us to love, the hands that take those nails and build things with it. Maybe even bridges.

BR

Hold the nails in your hands. What do they say to you?

Spotting God...

In Telemarketing

I am about to break the code—like a magician sharing the secret of his sleight or a fraternal brother divulging the distinctive nature of a hand-shake. I recognize that I may incur the wrath of every former and present prepubescent male, but the time has come. This breach of sacred secrets is prompted by my need to make amends—on all our behalves—to the ministers of music who have frantically flailed their arms before us in an effort to get us to sing together. Well, here goes.

We "back-pew boys" have been massacring hymn lyrics for decades. Our parents have watched us from the choir loft. They have gleamed with pride as they observe our smiling faces projecting sound at the top of our lungs. In the communal roar of the congregation, however, they could not hear our specific voices and vocalizations—thank God.

What back-pew boy has not sung (to the tune of "At the Cross")...

> At the bar, at the bar, where I smoked my first cigar
> And the fumes of smoke rolled away (rolled away).
> It was there, by chance, that I tore my Sunday pants,
> And now I have to wear them every day.

Or (to the tune of "The Old Rugged Cross")

> On a hill far away, stood an old Chevrolet,
> Its tires all tattered and torn.
> But I loved that old car...

And, of course, that popular Easter classic (to the tune of "Low in the Grave He Lay")

> Up from the grave he arose
> With a great big pickle in his nose...

(Settle down; it's only a hymnal, not the Bible.)

And finally (to the tune of "Lead On, O King Eternal")

Lead on, O Kinky Turtle
(I'm not sharing the rest of those lyrics)

Last week, a telemarketer contacted me at the church office. He was selling video/sound systems for worship centers (his language, not mine). I told him we leaned a little more liturgical and had no need for the system. He quickly countered, "Dr. Dant, these systems give us the ability to feel the spirit of God without having to fumble with pages and papers. As choruses, scriptures, and outlines are projected on one single screen, we can corporately focus on this fixed point, and the Spirit is better able to unite us as a body. Any church interested in experiencing spiritual and numeric growth would welcome these tools and methods of ministry."

I further explained that I have never been critical of such tools and methods; I refuse to take up arms in the worship wars. But I truly believe that people experience God and express their love for God in a multitude of ways. I am happy that other churches offer these avenues of praise. However, our church has enjoyed an influx of new members over the last decade—most are young adults with young children, seeking to reunite with the traditional rituals of the faith. I ended my comments by inviting him to attend one of our services to get a taste of our style of worship. He told me he wasn't particularly religious and had not attended church since he was a child. At that moment, I think God shed a tear.

I also believe God chuckles at back-pew boys who massacre hymns. God knows you're only teased if you're loved.

JD

How have you "acted out" in church, and how might that have brought joy to the life of God?

Spotting God...

On Posterboard

My harvest moon-colored Volkswagen convertible rolled to a stop where Craddock Way meets Rivoli Drive in Macon, Georgia. Affixed to the stop sign on my right was a lost dog poster. Clear packing tape wrapped the permanent-marker-inked white posterboard to the metal pole. It read,

LOST DOG

Dachshund

Red

May be injured

If found, please call

###-###-####

I always read these signs. On my list of "100 Things to Do before I Die" is to find a lost dog and return it to their owner. I've just always thought that would be a cool thing to do. I can only imagine how good it would make me feel.

The next morning, I'm sitting at our breakfast table in the nook of a bay window overlooking our backyard, and what do I see limping along in the woods behind my house? A red dachshund! I leap to my feet, grab my dog's leash from its designated hook on the key holder, and run to the backyard. At first, the car-struck canine didn't trust this wild-eyed, self-gratification-seeking hero. But the toss of a few dog biscuits instituted a true friendship. To make a long story short, I leashed the pup, dialed the number, and eventually handed the furry little friend over to a teary-eyed, grateful family. There was no monetary reward. I needed none. The moment was as sweet as I had imagined. And I marked the moment off my list.

It's the feeling for which J. D. Salinger's Holden Caulfield was longing when he said,

> Anyway, I keep picturing all these little kids playing some game in this big field of rye and all. Thousands of little

kids, and nobody's around—nobody big, I mean—except
me. And I'm standing on the edge of some crazy cliff.
What I have to do, I have to catch everybody if they start
to go over the cliff—I mean if they're running and they
don't look where they're going I have to come out from
somewhere and catch them. That's all I do all day. I'd just
be the catcher in the rye and all. I know it's crazy, but that's
the only thing I'd really like to be. (*The Catcher in the Rye*)

Maybe it's the feeling people of faith experience when they are able to
help orient one lost sheep, one lost coin, or one lost child in the direction of
God.

JD

Get out there and do something nice for someone today.
Then write about the good feeling it generates inside of
you.

Spotting God...

In the Quick Step

I like to dance. I'll probably never be invited to appear on *Dancing with the Stars* or even participate in community musical theater. But I like to dance. I've never had formal training or been particularly coordinated in my informal attempts. But as a high school student I made a point to appear at all gyrational gatherings. In college I dated under the disco lights of Packets and the Limelight in Atlanta.

I had the opportunity to dance this past Saturday. I was ending a long run up Northside Drive in Macon. A shadow moved across the sidewalk in front of me. An overhanging limb or a darting bird seemed to be casting its sun-darkened image on the pale concrete of the sidewalk. At least that's what I thought. Stepping inches from the spastic splotch, I recognized the *elephae obsoleta obsoleta*—a black rat snake! He moved around my feet, and I spastically moved around him. We "danced."

Several years ago, I was sitting on the examining table of the emergency room at the George E. Weems Memorial Hospital in Apalachicola, Florida. "You have a kidney stone," the doctor finally reported.

"A kidney stone!" I exclaimed, while continuing to writhe in pain. "How will I know when it's gone?"

"Well," the doctor said, "It will move out of your kidney, hurt like Hades moving down your ureter, and when it hits your bladder, you'll perform the 'great kidney stone dance' until you expel it. It will be gone moments after the dance."

The doctor was right. I danced.

The best dances have nothing to with snakes or stones (unless maybe it's Whitesnake or the Rolling Stones); rather, they are the result of love. Having someone wrap their arms around you with a little Norah Jones or Gladys Knight or El DeBarge or Al Green or Marvin Gaye playing in the background. Swaying in a rhythm that lets you know you are held and loved and known.

Sometimes I dance in pain. Sometimes I dance in fear. I think love is the greatest dance. In a life filled with fears and pains, I love it when God cuts in.

JD

How have you danced with God—in fear or in love?

Spotting God...

Under an Umbrella

Life has been especially unkind to a dear friend of mine in the past few months. I was thinking about her a few weeks ago, wishing I could bind myself to her side for a while and we could face life together like a three-legged race. I wished for a mystical umbrella that I could hold over her, one that would shield her from the storm of sadness that was drenching her and protect her from the pelting hail of disappointment, making it a struggle even to stand.

But I didn't have an umbrella like that. So what could I do? I just loved on her as much as I could, and I prayed.

A couple days later, I was thinking about my friend again (which to me also means looking for God in nooks and crannies of thoughts about her), and I decided to go for a run and think about her some more. So I went. You won't believe what I found.

I should explain that people dump stuff along the little alley behind my house all the time, even after my husband put up two NO DUMPING signs. Most of the time it's stuff I don't want, like two dead beavers or a cabinet or an old desk (because who ever heard of Goodwill?).

But this thing I found on my run was just what I wanted! IT WAS AN UMBRELLA! I'M NOT EVEN KIDDING! It was a bit dirty and had the fabric removed, but that was fine because after I washed it off with a scrub brush and my garden hose, it was completely ready to be transformed into a PRAYER UMBRELLA!

But how does one transform a regular patio umbrella into a prayer umbrella? I had no idea, but I knew just who to ask: children. They'd know what to do. And they did! We decided to paint it first and then weave colorful fabric through the spokes. When that was done, they'd draw symbols of God and hope along with encouraging words: *God will give you rest. Love each other. God loves you. Trust God. God loves you no matter what.*

We'd tie these pictures and words to ribbons and hang them from the underside of the umbrella, and then we'd ask God to bless it so whoever stood underneath this love umbrella, this prayer umbrella, would remember how much God loves them. We'd put it in a stand where kids and adults could stand under it whenever they wanted, no matter what life was pelting them with, no matter what storm they were facing. Whether it was sorrow, disappointment, guilt, shame, or loss, underneath the umbrella they'll find a love shower of God. Our umbrella wouldn't stop the rain, but maybe it could grant folks a glimpse of the sun that shines above it. Maybe it could help them soak in the hope God offers.

Over the next few weeks, three small teams of children worked on it. Finally, it was done and ready for use. Would they go for it? I didn't know. After all, who ever heard of a prayer umbrella?

"It's a prayer umbrella," I told the children after their tummies were full of doughnuts and they were about to be dismissed for Sunday school. "So if you would like us to pray for you—or if you have someone you love who needs prayer—go right now to stand under it, and we'll say a prayer for you."

I held my breath for a second and then watched eight children of all different ages race over to it to stand underneath. "Now, before we pray you have the option of telling us what you'd like prayer for," I told them. "You don't have to, but if you'd like to, it will help us know what to pray for."

Most of them shared. There were pets that needed prayer, people whose grandmother or grandfather died and they were still sad about it, and people who knew people who were sick. "I'm standing here for Mrs. Carson," one child said, referring to her Sunday school teacher, "because I'm sure she's sad about her son and her granddaughter who died in the car accident."

"Yes," several children joined in. "Let's pray for her."

So our umbrella had a proper christening, if you want to call it that. I'll admit that as I led the kids in prayer, I couldn't resist opening my eyes, just for a second. I'm afraid that I'm greedy when it comes to seeing beautiful things, and this was truly stunning, all those bowed heads and eyes squinted shut, all those fervent prayers going up.

Who knew that with a prayer umbrella, when prayers go up, we'd all get soaked in love?

BR

Who needs to stand under your prayer umbrella today?
What messages or symbols would you hang above their
heads?

Spotting God...
In Muddy Knees

She must have been about my age at the time, around 19 years old, and as she led us past the thousands of crosses to my grandfather's grave at the military cemetery at Colleville-sur-Mer, France, I wished she'd just hand over the map and let us find it by ourselves.

First of all, there was the awkwardness of the language barrier. She spoke English, but so quietly and with such a heavy accent that we could hardly understand her. But mainly I was concerned about my mom. This would be the first time since she was a baby that she'd be mere feet from her father's body, now bones and dust under the green grass, and I didn't want her to have to think about keeping her composure just because a stranger was there.

Will she cry? I wondered. Of course she would. In my dream the night before, she'd lain face down over her father's grave, and when the camera shifted to a cross-section scene, I could see my mother lying over her father and, five feet below, his face looking up at hers through the soil.

Would I cry? Would my brother or my dad? I walked faster, hoping to get Dad's attention and maybe signal him to take the map and send the girl back. But he was too busy looking at Mom that I couldn't catch his eye.

It started to drizzle, and I hoped that maybe now she'd go back, hand us umbrellas, and let us go on our own. But no, she walked on, ignoring the weather, carrying the bucket of wet sand that she'd taken time to get before we started out. Couldn't that chore, whatever it was, have waited? I shivered in the wind, glad to have my jacket, and noticed her bare legs.

Finally, there it was, my grandfather's cross. My father inched closer to my mother, who stood still, transfixed by the name. Now she'll leave, I thought. Instead, the girl knelt before the cross, her bare knees sinking in the wet ground. What in the world? She dipped her hand into the bucket, pulled out a clump of wet sand, and began smearing it all over the cross! Wasn't Dad going to say something? The cross had been beautiful, and now it was a terrible mess.

40

Before I could think of what to say, the girl picked up a clean cloth and with slow, deliberate strokes wiped it clean. The cross was gleaming white, but now Glen Kuhn's name stood out in bold brown letters. His cross had been just one of thousands, but now it proclaimed my grandfather's service, for all to see.

As I tried to catch my breath, the girl stood, her knees muddied. She thanked my mother for her father's service and left us to be alone.

I've thought of that girl so many times over the last 32 years. I've remembered how she gathered her skirt and knelt on the wet ground, how she stroked the cross so reverently, honoring my grandfather and then our privacy. She wouldn't let the awkwardness of a language barrier stand in the way of her focus on our family. Maybe it was her job, but she performed the task as if it were a holy mission.

Over the years this stranger became a model for me of what it means to be a Christ-like servant: to show up, put away any concerns or thoughts of yourself, and be willing to sink your knees in the mud for someone who needs it.

BR

Has someone muddied their knees for you lately? Check yours out. They may be muddy too.

Spotting God...

In 4/4 Time

The evening worship session of summer youth camp had ended hours ago. Curfew had finally been enforced. With my sermon a mere memory, I was relaxing beside the campground pool, sipping an ice-cold Mr. Pibb, and watching the stars twinkle above the Atlantic. Mr. Music, my cohort in worship leadership, was sitting next to me—mahogany pressed against the flesh of bare belly—picking a melody. A conversation ensued.

"Hey, Jim, wanna hear a tune the Lord gave me this morning?"

Being a music lover, I quickly responded, "Sure, play it for me."

My buddy beat the steel strings of his Martin with a familiar 4/4 pattern. The I-V-IV chords fell in predictable sequence as he vocalized a melody. The twelve meditative words were repeated several times, and the chorus slowly resolved to the tonic.

"What did you think?" he asked.

With an affirming nod, I responded, "It was okay."

"Just okay? Just okay? What do you mean by 'okay'?"

"I mean it was okay. You're not going to win a Grammy Award, and it probably won't be the title cut to an album…it was okay."

"Well, if the Lord gave it to me, it has to be better than okay!" he defensively charged.

"Look," I explained, "you realize that many of the great composers attributed their work to 'heavenly inspiration.' Bach, for instance, wrote hundreds of works for the keyboard and many more for orchestra and choir. At one point in his career, he was writing a cantata a week for use in worship! A cantata a week! Some of his works are hours long and so musically intricate that they move the listener through a complete range of emotion and meditative experience. Nietzsche even wrote, after hearing the *St. Matthew Passion*, 'One who has completely forgotten Christianity truly hears it here as gospel.' I'm just saying, in light of all that, I think your tune is 'okay.' Okay?"

"So," he continued in a voice of dismay, "you're saying God didn't give me the tune."

"No," I said, as I stared out over the vast Atlantic, "I'm just saying God ain't working as hard as he used to."

JD

We don't have to be a Bach or a Beethoven to be used by God. What unique gift has God given you, and how are you using it to further God's kingdom?

Spotting God...

In a Wild Child

When you were little, what kind of person did you think God expected you to be?

I wish I had shared the outlook of a little boy I know. We recently celebrated the story of Jesus' baptism in Sunday school, and when the teacher asked "I wonder where *you* are in the story. I wonder what part of the story is about you," he gave a response I love.

"I'm like John the Baptist," he said, "because John was wild, and I'm wild sometimes."

I'm not sure if he meant wild as in a woodsy kind of guy who likes to eat bugs and sleep outside or wild as in a slightly mischievous guy who likes to sneak extra doughnuts before Sunday school, gobble them down in the corner, and then run circles around the air hockey table until the children's minister pulls him aside and lets him collect himself and come down off his sugar high. Not that I know anybody like that.

But either way is good for me. Either way the child is saying, "God picked a wild guy to do God's work. Yay! So God could pick me too!"

We can be wild and still be part of God's story. We don't have to be brave like David ALL THE TIME (he wasn't brave all the time either). We don't have to be faithful like Sarah ALL THE TIME (I'm sure she wasn't faithful all the time either). Because as much as we try—or don't try—we know nobody can be perfect all the time (well, nobody except one). We were made human, so we all have weaker, darker moments.

This gives me hope.

I'm so glad that our sacred stories are all about broken people pursued by God to be part of God's action in the world. And I'm glad for girls and boys who are wild and wise enough to see themselves as part of the story.

BR

When you were little, what kind of person did you think God expected you to be? Pick a favorite Bible story from your childhood. Are there traits you SOMETIMES share with these Bible heroes from days of old?

Spotting God...

Between the Lyrical Lines

Habakkuk was a musician—a one-hit wonder, but a musician nonetheless. Isaiah was a musician—the Servant Songs, which are scattered throughout his three-disc prophetic anthology, have become festive favorites for Christianity's most cherished feast days. Even Paul appreciated music. His epistle to the Philippians serves as liner notes to one of the oldest Christian hymns. And who can miss the fact that 150 songs sit at the center of our Christian canon?

In every generation, musicians speak for God—even when they are unaware. Their "revelation receptors" just seem to work better than other folks'. Here are a few lyrical lines that have stopped me in my musically meditative tracks. I'm sure you have a few of your own.

> Often times it happens that we live our lives in chains, and
> we never even know we have the key.
> > The Eagles, "Already Gone"

> I'm learning to say, "I'll be happy either way."
> > Ani DiFranco, "Educated Guess"

> I'd rather laugh with the sinners than cry with the saints.
> The sinners are much more fun.
> > Billy Joel, "Only the Good Die Young"

> If you can tell a wise man by the color of his skin, Mister,
> you're a better man than I.
> > Aerosmith, "Living on the Edge"

> I'm a hazard to myself.
> > Pink, "Don't Let Me Get Me"

I'd rather live in his world than live without him in mine.
Gladys Knight, "Midnight Train to Georgia"

Everybody hurts…sometimes. So hold on…hold on…
R.E.M., "Everybody Hurts"

Life is so brief, and time is a thief when you're undecided.
And like a fistful of sand, it can slip right through your
hands.
Rod Stewart, "Young Turks"

There ain't no Coupe De Ville hiding at the bottom of a
Cracker Jack Box.
Meat Loaf, "2 out of 3 Ain't Bad"

Living is easy with eyes closed, misunderstanding all you
see.
The Beatles, "Strawberry Fields Forever"

Why am I soft in the middle when the rest of my life is so
hard?
Paul Simon, "You Can Call Me Al"

All you touch and all you see is all your life will ever be.
Pink Floyd, "Breathe"

When my soul was in the lost and found, you came along
to claim it.
Carole King, "A Natural Woman"

I think it's about—forgiveness.

Don Henley, "Heart of the Matter"

Caught in a landslide, no escape from reality. Open your eyes, look up to the skies and see.

Queen, "Bohemian Rhapsody"

I guess that's enough for today.

JD

What musical lyric gives definition to your life and world?

Spotting God...

In the Cornfield

If it'd been up to her, I'm sure Janice never would have hired me. She needed a girl with arm muscles, someone tough enough to tramp through cornfields in the blazing summer heat, to dig holes 18 inches deep with only a hand auger, collecting thousands of samples of soil to analyze for Janice's graduate thesis. Janice had trained for the work, lifting weights and running up hills in her work boots. At 17, my most athletic moments were the times I was accidentally hit by a ball while walking across my high school gym.

But Daddy and her advising professor were friends, so there I was in the state-owned truck at 4:30 a.m., smelling the diesel and her coffee as we headed off to yet another cornfield of eastern North Carolina. With temps in the upper nineties, 100% humidity, and at least 250 holes to dig each morning, Janice and I were always on the road early, racing against the elements.

"Eat a whole-wheat pumpkin muffin; it'll help," she'd say, and hand me the paper bag. Janice was the only person I knew in 1981 who ate yogurt and bought whole-wheat flour. "Your body is a machine," she'd say. "You've got to give it the right fuel."

Janice baked? How interesting that this lady in the tank top, shorts, and steel-toed shoes could be such a bizarre mix of my mother and my father. She did research with a team of men, yet she made up recipes of her own? Would I be like her when I was a worldly woman of 23?

Janice was a patient teacher, up to a point. She taught me to follow the maps she'd sketched off on graph paper, to count our paces as we walked down each row, the leaves slapping our faces, making paper cuts on our eyelids and cheeks. She taught me to squat as I twisted the auger through the soil, to use thigh muscles I didn't know I had. And on the few occasions when I didn't sweat out the gallons of water we downed, she taught me how to find a tree at the edge of a field, grab onto it, squat again, and pee.

When the days were especially unbearable, Janice would help me make an ice hat. We'd pack our floppy hats with ice and salt, then quickly turn them over and tie them on our heads. An hour later, we'd get punchy and fall over laughing at the sight of each other with the water dribbling down our necks, our faces smeared with dirt, our shirts soaked with sweat and melted ice. She'd tease me about turning from Little Miss Weakling into Wonder Girl, and I'd feel myself walk taller. And at the end of the day, when I'd dance around the truck, lost in the ecstasy that comes with finishing something hard, with pushing my body to the brink of exhaustion, I'd catch a smile on her face as she turned away, forcing herself to hold back the sarcasm. She was proud of me. I was sure of it.

But work with Janice wasn't all daisies and ice hats. Janice also taught me how to properly receive a cussing. One day she cussed at me for 15 minutes straight, combining cuss words in arrangements I'd never even heard before. We had just finished our second field of the morning, and I was in the throes of euphoria. We both were, laughing and singing and jogging back to the truck. Lunch was only 15 minutes away, at a restaurant with the coldest, sweetest iced tea in the entire state of North Carolina.

And then I tripped.

She cussed as we fumbled around in the dirt and gathered every one of the 250 canisters and lids. She cussed as she carried the crate back to the truck, and she cussed as I sat in the truck and cried dirty tears. Janice saw me crying and just kept cussing.

And then she stopped.

After a quiet moment at the back of the truck, Janice returned to my side, fished the graph paper map of the field out of her back pocket, clipped it back on her clipboard, and said, "We better get started. Got your water?" We started over, and that was the end of it.

It's funny. I've worked in laboratories and in high schools, in a kindergarten and in churches, but I count walking the cornfields with Janice as one of my best training grounds ever. Janice taught me that my body could do amazing things, that I could work harder than I ever thought possible, for longer than I ever imagined. I learned that my sensitive nature was resilient too. Words were just words, and a person could be funny and loving in their own way and still cuss a blue streak. I learned that women can be tough and soft and hard and kind, all at the same time—or maybe at different times.

But the best lesson I learned with Janice was that I can find joy and even God in working my hardest at a difficult task, even if it's digging holes. I'm still trying to figure out how that works. Is it because we come from God? That when we push ourselves to really dig for strength and the abilities God gave us, we get more in touch with the source of strength? That God's own traits become more visible? I don't know. But I am certain that whenever I go through hard things and come out at the other end, I discover more about myself and the God who made me.

BR

Remember the hardest job of your life. What did it teach you about yourself as a child of God?

Spotting God...

Among the Bugs at Miss Minnie's House

Before I even opened her chain-link gate, I could see her legs in a wheelchair pulled up to her screen door. A wheelchair? Miss Minnie started using a walker a couple years ago, and in the last few months she'd moved slower with it, gripping it hard. I heard the buzz of flies. They were darting around the bag of garbage she had left on her porch, where I would have to stand.

I braced myself and walked on. "Hey there, Miss Minnie. It's Becky, with Meals on Wheels," I said, and she reached up from her chair to click open the lock.

"Hey," she said, her voice sounding weaker than usual. "You weren't here last time. Somebody else came."

"Yes, ma'am. My family went to the beach."

"Oh, that's nice."

I opened the door. She always keeps the lights off in hot weather, and today it was nearly 100 degrees. Once my eyes adjusted to the darkness, I tried not to shudder at the sight of her. Three years ago this woman was big-boned and vigorous, but now she seemed to have shrunk. What had happened? There were little red scabs all over her face. I looked down at the bugs scattering across her floor, then to the piles of things on her bed. There were bugs on the sheets too. Were the scabs from bug bites?

This made me angry. I'd already called the social worker, trying to convince her that, no, the filth wasn't her own fault, that THE WOMAN CAN'T SEE. Now she was worse off than before.

"How are you doing today?"

"Oh, I'm here. That's good enough, I guess."

"I brought your mail," I said. "Maybe somebody's sent you a check!" That's our long-running joke, that maybe one day there will be a check in her stack of bills.

Miss Minnie laughed. "Do you think you'd have time to help me read these too?" she asked, reaching for some mail on her bed.

"Sure," I made myself say, remembering that the last time I did this, bugs were feeding on the glue on the envelopes. Did I really have to do this? I remember when Meals on Wheels was just plain fun, when I could show up like meal Santa, knocking on doors, dropping off meals, and chatting with people. I consider saying, "I'm sorry, Miss Minnie. I can't today." But she has no one.

"Why don't you come on in?" she said as she backed up her wheelchair a foot until it bumped against her bed.

"That's okay," I said, staying in the doorway. "I don't want to crowd you." I felt ashamed, but I didn't want to go in her house any farther. It smelled, and I kept imagining rats.

"Looks like you got a package," I said, holding up a puffy envelope.

"Oh, yeah. That's probably my gun."

What? "A gun?"

"Yeah," Miss Minnie laughed, enjoying my shock. "It's one of those tester things. For my diabetes." We laughed some more as I pulled at the envelope. I said I thought she meant a real gun, and she said she'd thought about buying one with all the break-ins lately. I told her she'd better not do that, that somebody would only use it against her. Finally, I managed to rip the package open.

"Well, let's see what you've got here," I said, reaching in. Wrapped in plastic wrap was a box of toothpaste, a new toothbrush, and a travel package of tissues. I handed it to her and told her what it was. "There's a card," I said and read it to her: "For Minnie, We're thinking of you and hope you're doing well. We love you. Love, Your Church Family."

❦

We looked at each other for a moment, neither knowing what to say. "Well," she said as I handed her the card, "isn't that helpful." She looked up at me, and we laughed a little.

I looked down at her sitting in the wheelchair, scabs all over her face, bugs crawling over both our shoes, a chamber pot by her bedside, the lights out. I saw her cradling the toothpaste and toothbrush and tissues in her lap, laughing her weak little laugh.

I wanted to cry. And I wanted to shake someone. I wanted to shake her niece, who knows full well that she's the only one Miss Minnie has in the whole wide world, yet she lets her live that way. I wanted to shake her church, a mere half mile away, for staying in the air conditioning and mailing out toothpaste when she lives in such a desperate state. But mostly I wanted to shake myself, that even now, I wanted so badly to run out of there, get in my car, and zoom back to my clean, bug-free life, to a hot shower and antibacterial soap.

I think of Jesus, healing the lepers, putting mud on blind eyes, touching and touching and touching again, and I'm sad that I fall so short.

So I make myself stay a few more minutes, thanking God for the chance to know Miss Minnie and her wry sense of humor and for the chance to try to be Jesus' hands, just for a little while, before I go home and start making phone calls.

BR

*Have you encountered places where it's difficult to serve,
where you want to forget it and run?*

Spotting God...

In the Pew Pocket

As a pastor I rarely get to enjoy the perspective of the pew. Each Sunday, I typically sit in a "reserved seat" just left of the pulpit, facing the congregation. I don't think anyone minds me sitting there. I'm not sure anyone else wants the seat. No one has ever been sitting there when I entered the sanctuary to sit down. Like a lot of parishioners, I guess I have my "usual seat" in the sanctuary.

Recently, however, hosting a guest speaker forced me to forego my standard seating arrangement. I sat in the pew—like a normal person. It was really a great seat. I could see the choir, Communion table flowers, organ pipes, and soloist. I even had an array of reading material available in the pew pocket in front of me (there is no chair in front of my usual seat, therefore, no pew pocket). While the guest speaker eloquently pontificated about something, I foraged the file before me (I think this is similar to what normal parishioners do). I read through welcome cards, prayer request cards, someone's discarded Alcoholics Anonymous bookmark, and about three different designated offering envelopes.

It was the offering envelopes that started my daydreaming (which, again, is similar to what normal parishioners do). Many churches promote seasonal offerings for various causes: Christmas and Easter offerings for missions, Mother's Day offerings for children's homes, a Gideon offering for Bibles—well, you know the drill. In my daydreams, I thought it would be nice if people of faith throughout the nation—I'm talking Christians, Muslims, Jews, Hindus, and everything outside and in between—instituted a July 4 offering for the nation (hear me out). On the Sunday nearest July 4, a special collection would be taken to pay off the national debt. Each gift would be tax-deductible—since it's going through the religious institutions—and it would benefit every citizen as well as their children and grandchildren. It would give everyone a positive way to express their patriotism and concretely convey a little hope. Now, I had some critics in my daydream: "I already pay enough taxes"; "the government got themselves into this mess; they need to get themselves out,"; "if we give them the money, they'll just waste it." Most of the arguments, however, could be made about most of our financial situations. But wouldn't it be nice to be debt-free?

I was never real comfortable with "faith-based grants." I just had a problem with the government giving the church money—as if God needs anyone's assistance to accomplish God's work in the world. I'm pretty comfortable, however, with the faithful sharing a gift with the government. What if people of faith actually saved the nation? Wow, what a thought.

So I'll be back in my usual chair next week, wondering whether or not to share my daydream with the fiscally conservative congregation that faces me each week, daydreaming their own daydreams. I'm willing to pursue this idea, however. Anybody with me? Anybody have the president's phone number so we can get the executive office on board? Anybody tight with a congressperson who could help us get the word out? Okay, maybe it's a bad idea.

JD

Where does your money go, and how does it glorify God and minister to God's world?

Spotting God...

In the Parking Lot

I was standing in the parking lot at Target, melting into the asphalt while my son ran back to the car for his wallet, when I realized a young woman was talking to me. "I hate those things," she said, nodding at the stick-figure family decal on the back of somebody's SUV. She must have thought I was staring at it.

"Yeah?"

"Yeah," she nodded. "Mommy scorecard."

Mommy scorecard? I'd seen those decals all around town, stick-figure mommies and daddies and lines of kids. Sometimes they'd tote soccer balls or wear ballet tutus, and cats and dogs always trailed behind.

Now, be aware that stick-family stickers are fine with me. If you want to celebrate each member of your family, why not? Peel and stick away. But I admit that the mommy scorecard part strikes a chord. Too often, I've pulled up next to others in the parking lot of life and checked out how we compare. Did we have the complete package: the happy couple, the full set of kids with smiles on their faces, pompoms and flutes in hand?

When I was a younger mom, home with a two-year-old and a newborn while Todd traveled constantly with work, people would see Ben spitting up on my shoulder and Sarah tugging on my jeans and say, "I don't know how you do it, night after night, by yourself."

I'd paw a foot at the floor and do my best *"Aw, it's no big deal,"* and then I'd casually work in a comment about the grad school class I was taking or the volunteering I had to do. It made me feel good for a moment, for someone to recognize my hard work and exhaustion, the perfect picture I was trying to project. But I'd always end up feeling empty when the conversation was over.

We want people to see us as complete and successful. Sometimes we tout our own completeness and success and possessions loudly—we sneak them into conversations or wear them like sandwich boards—because underneath it all, we know the truth: that we don't really have it all together. Life isn't the perfect picture we want to paint.

As I tuck the scorecard in my purse, I also wonder about those of us who don't match up to the picture on the window, whether through choice or circumstance. The single person, the couple that looks different or doesn't have the urge to go forth and multiply. The pair that wants children desperately, but life is cruel and won't cooperate. The families that fall apart. I hope they know the truth that I'm still learning, that God loves us as we are, whether we match the world's ideal or not, whether we do the volunteer work or just sit in front of the TV. That our sad little efforts to mold ourselves to the perfect picture in our heads won't make God love us any more than God already does. God only asks us to do what Galatians advises:

> Make a careful exploration of who you are and the work
> you have been given, and then sink yourself into that....
> Don't compare yourself with others. Each of you must take
> responsibility for doing the creative best you can with your
> own life. (Gal 6:4, The Message)

Do the creative best you can with your own life. That's a tall order, but I'm working on it.

BR

If you put a true picture of your stick-figure family on your window, warts and all, what would it look like? Take a good look at all your imperfections, and let God pour God's love on you anyway.

Spotting God...

In the Hardcore

John Dahlz was the overall winner of the 2012 Vineman Ironman on Saturday, July 28. He swam 2.4 miles in the Russian River (half against the current and half with) in less than 49 minutes. I took exactly an hour longer. He biked 112 miles on the hilly roads of Napa Valley in 4 hours and 57 minutes. I rode the same course in 8 hours. He ran the 26.2-mile three loops through the back roads of Windsor, California, in 3 hours and 52 minutes. I ran—walked much of it—in a painful 6 hours and 30 minutes. Most of us would agree that John Dahlz is a hardcore athlete.

I was way too sick to have begun this race, but I had trained too long and too hard to walk away from the start line. Four days before the race I contracted a sore throat, which turned into a chest cold, which—by race day—had gone full-blown head cold. Amazingly, I was able to cough and spit and blow my way through the swim and bike legs with little discomfort. But by mile three of the run, the sickness overwhelmed me. It was like having the flu...times ten! Determined to finish, I trudged on. By mile 15, my pace had slowed to the point that I knew I would not make the time cutoff required to begin loop three. The thought of quitting entered my mind, but I walked on. When I actually missed the cutoff—and knew I would be officially listed as DNF (did not finish)—the embryonic thought of giving up grew. A friend, who had accompanied me to the race, simply asked me, "Do you want to finish?" and then offered to walk the last eight miles with me. My only sane thought seemed to be, "Who quits a 140.6-mile race with only eight miles to go?" Coughing, straining and puking, I dragged myself through the final miles. To my surprise, the finish area was not empty when I arrived. I crossed the finish line, and a volunteer draped a medal around my neck, handed me a finisher's t-shirt, gave me a hug, and said, "You are an Ironman." John Dahlz finished his race in 9 hours and 29 minutes. It took me almost 17 hours and 30 minutes.

This was not the way I'd dreamed the day would go. In some ways it was an uglier finish than I had imagined. I am a runner. I worried for weeks about the swim and the bike. I knew, however, that once I got to the run, I was in my element. I had envisioned—over and over again—sprinting across the finish. In other ways, however, it was a beautiful finish. A long walk with a friend and fellow warriors, the grace and true understanding of finish line volunteers, and the knowledge that even when the world—or at least the race officials—tell you you're beat, you can keep going. It has been said that when you've finished an Ironman, you have the strength to tell the rest of the world to go to hell. It's true. Reflecting on my journey—months of training, hours in the pool, miles on the bike, step after step after step of running, and 17-plus hours facing down every demon I have—I really don't give a damn that the results page of a website labels me as DNF. I finished. Even when it seemed I had no legitimate reason to finish, I finished. I am an Ironman.

I wasn't the only athlete waging war in the darkness. Keeping pace with me was a lady carrying an inhaler, fighting asthma for the last eight miles. Others were on the course limping—impaired along the way by injury or cramps. Others had missed time cutoffs for other reasons, but were pressing on—silently, slowly, steadily—determined to be Ironmen and Ironwomen. Suddenly, it was an honor to be among such a crowd. A lot of people would say John Dahlz is a hardcore athlete—and he is. But the unknown hardcore athletes were the ones who pushed their bodies into the late hours of a cold night and finished the course, not for prize money, but for the pride of knowing we could finish—Ironmen and Ironwomen.

JD

When has God helped you persevere in the past? What struggle is currently testing the levels of your strength and faith?

Spotting God...

In Jokes

When you come home from church on Sunday with your jaws sore from gritting your teeth, it's a good idea to question why. The answer one particular day had the face of my fourth-grader, Sam. What had possessed me to agree to teach his Sunday school class? I knew the moment he finished offering our closing prayer that it was time to have a talk.

I waited until Sunday lunch was over and he was full and mildly happy, and then I pleasantly announced that we needed to have a conversation.

"About what?"

"About your prayer in Sunday school."

Sam had volunteered to do the closing prayer, and at the time I was glad for him to do it. When I offer the prayer, I usually make a blanket statement like "Help everyone we mentioned who is sick, and be with our pets." This is because the children LOVE to participate with prayer requests, and along with the more serious requests, they tell us all about friends of friends who have colds, neighborhood dogs and cats who might be lost or coughing up too many hairballs, and people who threw up in class and how even the custodian got nauseous to see what they did. Our prayer list can be VERY LONG. But before we bow our heads, Sam always takes the time to go back through everyone's prayer requests and makes sure he gets all the names again so he can properly ask God for help—except this time he added something I thought was unnecessary.

"What was wrong with my prayer?"

"Nothing was wrong with it," I said. "It's just that when you stopped in the middle and said, 'Let's give it up to you for the sunny weather' and then said, 'Can I hear a "booya," people?' and several kids chimed in 'booya,' I just thought that was not appropriate."

Sam wrinkled his forehead. "Why?"

"Because it sounded like you were just trying to get attention."

"I WASN'T TRYING TO DO THAT! I wasn't! It was sunny. Don't you think we should thank God for sunny weather?"

"Of course I do. But why do you have to say it like that? Why can't you just say, 'Thank you for the sunny weather'?"

"Because that's boring. Don't you think that with all the sick grandmas and George's lost cat, God could use a laugh?"

"Well, yes, but…"

Sam sighed and put his hands on his hips. "Come on, Mom. You know I made God laugh."

"Sam."

"Mom, you know I did!"

What can I say? I guess he's right. Maybe God does need a laugh.

Booya.

BR

Think back on your time at church. What have you seen or heard that surely tickled God's funny bone?

Spotting God...

Making Footprints
in the Sand

I never run on the beach. Even while vacationing in coastal regions, I've always chosen the pavement over the sand. I'm used to pavement. I regularly run on pavement. Pavement is familiar. Today, however, I laced my shoes and hit the shore.

I ran an out-and-back, which is exactly what it sounds like. You leave from a particular point, run a prescribed distance or time, turn around, and run back on the same path. Today's run was scheduled for 12 miles—six miles out and six miles back.

Having never run on the beach, I quickly learned to avoid the soft sand. The footing in soft sand was difficult, and it created a strain on the calves. The harder sand allowed more speed and surety of footing. I also avoided the water's edge. People who stroll on the beach like to get their feet wet. Wet running shoes make for a soggy run. After the first six miles, I turned—as planned—and began to make my way back to the rented residence. As I ran, however, I saw that there were two sets of footprints in the sand where I had run out, and now there was only one set of footprints on the run back.

"Why, Lord?' I prayed. "Why were there two sets of footprints when I was running away, but now only one set of footprints as I make my way back?"

"Because," replied the Lord, "the girl you've been following at a safe, non-creepy distance—the one with the little pink shorts and matching sports bra—did not turn around when you turned around, you licentious idiot!"

After pausing for a moment of thoughtful self-awareness, I replied, "Oh…"

Okay, so my "footprints in the sand" meditation isn't as pious as that other one. But there is still much to be learned from my experience. First, the soft way isn't always the best way. Sometimes the hard route is the way to go. Second, thank God for the little things that make the long journey of life a little easier—a little more enjoyable. Sunrises, beaches, ocean waves, the sound of seagulls overhead and the sound of a favorite song stuck in your head...while you're running the hard path.

JD

When has a hard path been a profitable path on your journey?

Spotting God...

In the Big Blind

I was ordained to the gospel ministry in 1982. At that time I filled the pulpit of Parkwood Hills Baptist Church in Decatur, Georgia. In the years that followed, I enjoyed three decades of uninterrupted Sundays in the pulpits of Baptist churches. On Sunday, February 12, I preached my last sermon as a parish pastor—at least for a while.

This past Sunday, February 19, was my first Sunday out of the pulpit in three decades. What to do? I flew to Las Vegas, Nevada. At 8:00 o'clock on Sunday morning (when I'm usually knotting my tie and printing my sermon), I walked into the poker room of the Monte Carlo Hotel and Casino and signed up for the casino's no-limit Texas hold 'em poker tournament. An hour later, I was seated at the table and the first cards were dealt.

For the next three hours, I traded pew sitters for poker players. Instead of leading the blind, I was throwing blinds into the pot. As the hands were dealt, I won a few and lost a few—not much different than church work. At times, I felt I was too easy to read. That was true in the pastorate, however. I never held my cards very close during my pastoral ministry. People typically knew my hand when it came to issues like homosexuality, interfaith issues, church/state relations, universalism, and the like. I folded several times in the early years of ministry (not certain my hand would hold up against what others held), but in later years I played the cards I was dealt and was confident of their value.

The tournament ended a little after noon, and the rumor is true: I won! Yep. I didn't place second or third or thirtieth. I won! And just in case you were wondering, I entered the evening tournament that began at 11:00 p.m. I was interested in determining if my earlier success had been a fluke or a result of beginner's luck. I placed second in the evening tournament.

Maybe I heard God wrong thirty years ago (maybe I missed my calling?). Or maybe God was simply allowing me to relax and enjoy what might otherwise have been a lonesome and awkward day.

JD

What "worldly activity" has provided some otherworldly insight for you?

Spotting God...

In a
Well-Paced World

I was a longtime fan of the black rotary-dial phone. I liked the way my fingers felt when swirling in the smaller circles of the dial. I was enamored with the bright white numbers and letters that curved perfectly within each hole. I enjoyed the unique sound of both the clockwise push and the counter-clockwise return of the dialing mechanism. I loved the look of that phone on an end table. Push-button dialing was years old before I allowed one of those machines in my home. It took even longer to adapt to the idea of a cordless phone.

In recent years I've struggled with the evolution of mobile phones. The earliest versions were too big and a little too uppity. Only people with important jobs or extreme emergencies would need to carry such a monstrosity. However, as these contraptions became more portable, affordable, and common, I succumbed. I even purchased one for each of my three daughters (for emergencies only—although last month, according to our bill, they endured over 1,000 minutes of emergency phone conversations and over 700 emergency texts!). Several months ago, I went to our local phone vender to replace my broken flip phone with no camera. I informed the perky little clerk that I only made phone calls and needed a phone for no other reason. I left with an iPhone. It now rules my world.

I expect no recognition for my slow advancement. I expect no one to stand and applaud. There are hundreds of other folk just like me who stay behind the times. And when we finally catch up with those of you who have enjoyed the ease of such inventions, well, we do it quietly, almost regretting the time we lost without such amenities.

It was recently announced that the Southern Baptist Convention—the nation's largest Protestant denomination—is poised to elect its first African-American president after 167 years of following Christ. I'm beginning to understand what Jesus meant when he told the religious leaders that prostitutes and tax-collectors would enter the kingdom of heaven before them. People of faith are too often behind the progressive graces of a well-paced world.

The Cooperative Baptist Fellowship is two decades old. In its short history the fellowship has had male, female, clergy, lay, Asian, Caucasian, African-American, young, and old national moderators. Glad to be where I am—and wondering where we might need to pick up our pace.

JD

In your life, what institutions or systems are in need of a little change? How might you work to make them more graceful and just?

Spotting God...

In Crowd Surfing

I've often wondered what it might feel like to crowd surf—you know, like you see at concerts when someone lets himself be picked up by the crowd and passed overhead from person to person, face up, as if floating on an ocean of people? It must take trust (or brain-altering chemicals) to let yourself be lifted and passed like that.

Actually, maybe I do know how it feels.

I met a friend for coffee recently, and as we talked, I remembered an especially difficult time in my life. "It's not how I hoped my faith would be," I said. "I knew it would happen to me some day, that sorrow and terrifying fear would visit me too. Why wouldn't it? I expected at some point to face a life-or-death crisis, but when I'd imagined what it might be like, I don't know," I said, feeling my eyes well up. "When it did come, I didn't react how I thought I would."

My friend nodded, listening generously, not rushing me or trying to squeeze in words.

"I guess I thought that when it did happen, I would lock arms with God and spring out of the murk into the light. It wasn't like that at all."

"What was it like?"

"I couldn't even pray. I thought I'd stay in constant communication with God, but instead I felt a stoniness. I just focused on getting through each hour. God wasn't as much a presence as a motor in me, pulling me up from the floor to my hands and knees, helping me crawl from one moment to the next. But I knew God was there, even if I didn't hear words."

"Even if you didn't talk to God, you trusted," she said. "That's trust."

"Maybe," I said. "I guess that's what it was. I didn't feel capable of much else but trust. And if I could trust, it's only because I knew that my circle of friends would pray even when I couldn't. I felt the quiet inside me, and I knew where it had come from. They were lifting me up, passing me around, offering me and my family to God. I was so thankful for their prayers."

They were lifting me up, offering me and my family to God. Yes, I think I do know what crowd surfing feels like. It's a beautiful thing.

BR

Have deep sorrow and fear visited you too? Did you feel God's presence? How did others help you?

Spotting God...

In Silver Dollars

Last fall, I fell in love with the plant known as "silver dollars." You can find them at craft stores in the dried flower section, or you can meet me in the alley behind my house and I'll show you thousands. I'm afraid that's partly my fault. In order to reveal the silvery, translucent disks that look like cellophane silver dollars, one must peel off the ugly crackled circles enclosing them and the seeds they carry. I find it oddly satisfying, so as I walk, I peel. I'm afraid I'm the Johnny Appleseed of silver dollars. Sorry, neighbors, but at least it's just our alley.

Funny thing, then, when I went for a walk a few weeks ago and discovered a new spring plant had taken over. Purple flowers had come from nowhere, and now they were EVERYWHERE. Who knew that underground, beneath the silver dollars, these flowers were waiting to emerge?

After my walk I Googled the plant. And guess what? The purple flowers, the ones with the blooms like little crosses, were the exact same plant as the silver dollars! They weren't underground, waiting to emerge. They were right there in front of me, silver dollars, but in another stage. It was another beautiful form of the same plant.

I thought about silver dollars the last time I watched someone wield a Bible verse taken out of context as a weapon to support his distaste for peacemaking. "But it's in the Bible!" he said. "I'd put my money on it." Use a silver dollar, I thought. It might remind him that just as we need to see the entire plant to understand it, we also need to examine the entire Trinity to understand God. Ask Jesus what he thinks of peacemakers. He calls them blessed.

You know what else I love about silver dollars? It's part of the mustard family. You remember what Jesus said about the mustard seed, right? Maybe the kingdom of God could be like a silver dollar seed, which an unsuspecting walker scattered as she walked her dog in the alley behind her house. Though it is the smallest of all seeds, when it grows, it is the largest of garden plants and becomes a tree so that the birds come and perch in its branches.

Okay, so it's not a tree, so let's turn to the real parable. The kingdom of God is like a great tree, big enough for all us birds, with our broken wings and our affinity for simplifying the complex and complicating the simple. Creator God, Jesus, and Holy Spirit, reveal yourself among the branches. We need all three forms of you!

BR

Think of a verse you've heard taken out of context to use as a weapon. Ask Creator God, Jesus, and the Holy Spirit to help you look at it from all sides. What do you hear them say?

Spotting God...

In Beautiful Feet

It had to be the worst pickup line I'd ever heard at State. The guy sauntered over from his circle of friends in lounge chairs by the pool, stared at me standing there in my bathing suit, and yelled over his shoulder, "Guys, you're right! Her feet are ugly!" While my brain tried to take in the magnitude of his rudeness, he reached out his hand. "No, no," he said. "You've got it all wrong. You just proved our theory. Pretty girls always have ugly feet."

Thirty years later, I'd like to go back and give that whole group of Neanderthals a good thumping with my tote bag. And while I'm there, I'd bop my own self over the head that I let his stupid comment shock me into both a complex about my feet and a sick thrill to be publicly declared pretty. Ugh, college Becky, get some confidence please.

But the part about ugly (or beautiful) feet has me thinking about a passage from Isaiah.

How beautiful on the mountains are the feet of those who bring good news, who proclaim peace, who bring good tidings, who proclaim salvation, who say to Zion, "Your God reigns!" Listen! Your watchmen lift up their voices; together they shout for joy. When the Lord returns to Zion, they will see it with their own eyes. Burst into songs of joy together, you ruins of Jerusalem, for the Lord has comforted his people, he has redeemed Jerusalem. (Isaiah 52:7-9)

But what does this have to do with my life? With your life? It's about Babylon, right? How a messenger comes to the Jewish people and shares the great news that they can go home again, that after years of exile, God has not forgotten them! The men on watch see him running through the mountains, ready to share the news, and they break into song. His running feet are the prettiest sight they can remember!

But still, what does this have to do with today? With the things we're worrying and arguing about?

Do you know messengers who bring good news? People like Christ, who spend their lives in prayer and thought but won't let that be the end of it? Who can't be content to just stand around in their sandals but have to get off their couches and do something? People who are willing to take a running start, facing mountains that look too big to climb, to share God's message of hope and the value of life?

I think of my next-door neighbor from childhood, Mrs. Cliffornia Wimberly, a loving, strong, witty woman who was willing to run up the mountain of racial tension of the early 1970s. At a time when the school board was predominately male and white, this African-American lady had good news to share that we're all God's children and deserve the best environment to learn.

I think of Lyla Kloos, who ran up the mountain wearing an apron and carrying suitcases, making sure that college kids on mission trips (even those same Neanderthals) had good food to eat and encouragement that grown-ups other than their parents cared about them.

And I think of my sweet uncle, Jeff Farley, who ran up the mountain even with all his health challenges, taking in foster children with his wife Lois, giving them a chance to find out what family is all about.

How beautiful are the feet of God's messengers, indeed!

BR

Who are the beautiful mountain runners in your life?

Spotting God...

In Broken Ankles and Atticus Finch

It had been nearly three months since Angie missed a stair on a Florida vacation and her body and life took a wild tumble. Her ankle was broken in three places, and so were all her daily routines. Grandma moved in to help with the surgery, two different casts, a walker, crutches, and then a boot. How long would this go on? In a quiet moment her youngest son, Aidan, turned to his dad and asked, "When is Mom going to get over her brokenness?"

I love the question. When I first heard it, it spawned another: Do we *ever* get over our brokenness?

But I know where Aidan was coming from. Parents aren't supposed to be broken. They are the fixers.

My mom loves to tell the story of how when I was a toddler and anything was broken, I'd always shrug my shoulders and say, "Daddy fick it." My daddy could fix anything. I'd give the pieces to him to hold, he'd breathe his healing breath over them, and (abracadabra) it was fixed. Or so it seemed to me.

Then I started growing up. And as I grew in mind and body—and in my ability to break things or have others break me—I found out the terrible truth that even if they're engineers or magicians or have a closet full of superglue, parents can only do so much. I flopped my body over theirs and sobbed—or maybe I yelled at them instead because yelling's more comfortable—because I wanted them to fix it, fix me, fix whatever, and it wasn't working out like it used to do.

And then I kept growing and yelled some more because I discovered an even bigger, more terrible secret that really got me steamed: my parents were broken too! It wasn't just me. THE PEOPLE IN CHARGE ARE BROKEN! Who told them they could be broken? How is the world supposed to work now?

I'm not mad anymore, because I'm a long way from teenage-hood. I've watched the anger-storm swell in my own kids as they have discovered the terrible, horrible secret of my own brokenness and that of others around them. I've grieved with them when their heroes slipped off their pedestals, and I've watched them explore with dark fascination the weaknesses of adults, including myself, pushing our buttons, waiting to see the sharp edges of brokenness pop out of our insides when they cross the line. It's all normal, and my kids are really nice people. It's just something they have to do.

Maybe my acceptance of my own brokenness is part of why I'm crazy over Harper Lee's "new" book, *Go Set a Watchman*. I held back from reading it for a good while because Atticus Finch was my secret boyfriend, and I heard that if I read it, I'd have to witness all sorts of ugly things said about him, and I liked him on his *To Kill a Mockingbird* pedestal just fine. Finally, I gave in, and I'm glad I did. *Go Set a Watchman* allows us to watch Jean Louise discover her father's brokenness. As her uncle tells her near the end, "As you grew up…you confused your father with God. You never saw him as a man with a man's heart, and a man's failings—I'll grant you it may have been hard to see, he makes so few mistakes, but he makes 'em like all of us." It didn't make me love Atticus any less. It made me understand him more. (I still love you, Atticus. We have things to discuss, but I love you.)

Do we *ever* get over our brokenness? I don't think so. We can ask God for help, give God our pieces, let God hold them in his holy hands, let God breathe his healing breath over them. God still loves us—even when we're still not "fixed." We can't expect God to take away our humanness. But God meets us at the table, in bread and wine, with open arms, ready to hold us anyway.

BR

Who has been knocked from a pedestal in your life? Are you finding that you're able to love them, broken as they are, as God loves us?

Spotting God...

In
Fickleness

I just finished a six-mile run on the streets of Columbus, Ohio. Buckeye fever is evident in almost every shop window, on every car bumper, and on every piece of clothing. The NCAA Final Four is a bit convicting for me.

After moving from Arkansas, I attended high school in western Kentucky and adopted the Wildcats as my favorite basketball team. Later, spending three years in Louisville—like many young Baptist seminarians in the good old days—turned me into a University of Louisville fan. Recently, my oldest daughter completed a graduate degree at THE Ohio State University, so I'm visiting her in Columbus today and rooting for the Buckeyes tomorrow. I'm fickle; I admit it!

Growing up in the ArkLaMiss (the tristate delta of Arkansas, Louisiana, and Mississippi), it was required I support the New Orleans Saints when watching professional football (I was also told Archie Manning was my third cousin twice removed by an aunt-in-law). But I became enamored with Joe Namath and quickly claimed independence from the Saints, defecting to be a New York Jets fan. As a college student I moved to Atlanta and began following the faltering Falcons. And when it comes to college football, well, I've lived in Mississippi, Arkansas, Kentucky, and Georgia! I've made my way through the SEC like a football floozy! Currently living in Georgia, barking annoys me, buzzing barely sounds menacing, and I'm a Georgia State University alum. Again, I'm fickle! I really enjoy sports, but I'm not a diehard fan of any team. And that's okay. I don't want to die hard. I want to live freely and die gently.

In the last couple weeks, I've worshiped with a Presbyterian congregation and a Baptist congregation. Tomorrow morning, I'll be at a Saturday Mass. Sunday, I'm celebrating April Fool's Day with my Unitarian Universalist friends. Next week, it's Passover with a Jewish family and then Easter.

I really enjoy spending time with God and God's people, but I'm not a die-hard fan of any one team. In fact, I'm not interested in dying hard. I want to live freely and die gently—in the arms of a God who loves us all.

JD

Take a Sunday to visit a faith community other than your own. Make note of how God meets you there.

Spotting God...

In Dirty Verses

Nope, this is not an exegetical study of the Song of Songs or the music of the Red Hot Chili Peppers. It's actually a celebrative note for one more year of life.

Today is my birthday—September 22. This was not mentioned in order to garner gifts, cards, and well wishes (although none will be refused). And since it was my birthday, the good Lord shared a gift with me.

It all started yesterday. I rolled into my driveway after a long, arduous day of work (just in case any church members are reading this). I exited my car and noticed the neighbor's early elementary-aged child playing in the dirt between our yards. Dirt was on his face, hands, t-shirt, shoes—everywhere. He glanced my way. I nodded. He smiled and said, "I like dirt." I smiled and thought to myself, 'I'm glad you're not my kid and I don't have to clean the grit and grime and ringworms off of you tonight."

So...today is my birthday (I'm only trying to keep my rambling thoughts in context). I made my morning trek to the back deck for a little coffee and a conversation with God. I opened my devotional guide. Today's text? Psalm 90: "You turn men back into dust.... You sweep men away like a dream.... By evening they wither and fade." I was about to roll my eyes and thank God for the less-than-joyous-reminder of my fast-passing years, and then I saw the devotional writer's opening line—"We are only dust—but beloved dust!"

I paused, thanked God for his abundant love, and then thanked God for the abundant wisdom that resides in the mind and heart of that grimy kid next door.

JD

How have children conveyed God's love and nature to you?

Spotting God...

In Chemistry Class

Whenever it's time for school to start again, a certain memory of mine flies in for a visit and spends a few days fluttering like a moth around my brain, begging for attention. It was one of those pivotal, split-second moments in which you have to make a decision on how to react, and my choice doesn't exactly make me proud.

I was teaching chemistry at a high school, and it was the first day of class. I decided to start the year by doing a strange thing—strange, at least, to the other teachers and teens at my school. At each change of class, I stood outside my door in the noisy hall, and as students tried to duck their heads and dart into my classroom, I stopped them. I introduced myself to each student over the din and asked his name, welcomed him to the class, shook his hand, and showed him where to sit according to the seating chart on my clipboard.

Within seconds, a long line of young men and women had formed outside my door. "This is weird," I heard them say. "Why is she doing this?"

Why was I doing this? Partly to welcome them to my classroom. Partly to show my respect for them, the respect they got for free, respect that I required back. Partly, to be honest, to show dominance. I'm in charge of this class. It is my home (thus the curtains on the windows and the flowers on my lab table). I will respect you, but you must act like ladies and gentlemen in my classroom.

The teens watched me, watched their friends interact with me, waiting for something to happen. I knew this was weird for them. I expected that a few would try to amuse each other, tell me they go by the nickname "Trouble" or "Scooby-Doo," or tip their hat in fake formality, cushion the awkward earnestness of my handshake with sarcasm. I'd experienced it many times before and had learned to meet it head on, to set a businesslike tone on day one—friendly enough, but firm.

So far, the kids had been great. Then, a tall, red-headed boy made it to the front of the line, his eyes sparkling with mischief. "I'm Mrs. Ramsey," I said, thrusting out my hand. "Welcome to chemistry class." The boy shook

my hand, a corner of his lip turning up, as if he were about to spring something on me.

I waited for his name. He said nothing, just kept shaking my hand.
What was he doing?
"Now, tell me your name."

"I…I…" he said, looking hard at me. "My…" His mouth was open,
but nothing came out. Kids behind him snickered. "Go for it, Dan," one
boy said.

Time stopped.

What kind of joke was this? I could feel my body tensing, anger rising.
So he was one of those, huh? A kid who needs to impress his friends, to
start things off by showing me what a pain he'd be until I wrestled him into
control.

Other kids were watching. I'd give him one more chance to straighten
up. "I believe I asked for you to tell me your name."

He looked at me with his mouth open. "Now," I barked, my voice
dampened by the noise of the hall.

The student squinted his eyes at the floor, "Da Da Da Dan," he said.
"Dan At At At Atkinson."

My heart jumped into my throat. What had I done? He was stuttering.
He wasn't being rude or a smart aleck. He was struggling with a speech
problem, and I had exacerbated it, calling attention to it in front of everyone. "I'm glad to meet you, Dan," I said, trying to recover, wanting to
shrink into the linoleum. "You're in the third row from the door, second
seat."

Dan was doing his best, and I had assumed the worst.

Over the next few weeks, I quickly learned what a lovely person Dan
was. I still think of him from time to time and wonder how he's doing.

I'm not teaching anymore, and I hope I've grown a lot since then. So why does this memory always flutter back to my shoulder this time of year? Maybe God sends me this memory like the moth God wants me to be—not held down, locked by fear, but soaring high, believing I can be the generous person God made me to be. And if I fall—or if I'm struck down—God will be there to catch me.

BR

Do you have any back-to-school memories that don't make you proud? What do you think God would say to you about these memories?

Spotting God...

In Liquid Commodities

I pumped eight gallons of gasoline into the tank of my Volkswagen Beetle. I glanced at the convenience store marquee and noted that my petro was costing me $3.25 a gallon. I only glanced at the well-lit information because I really don't care. I have friends who religiously follow and fret and figure and grumble about gasoline-related issues. They know all about OPEC and guarded reserves and dollars per barrel and price fixing. Me? I just fill up and drive.

I shopped for printer ink yesterday. Now there's something that puzzles me. Next to printer ink, gasoline looks like a deal! I can purchase a whole gallon of gas for the low, low price of $3.25 per gallon. This gasoline has to be drawn from the belly of the earth, pumped through miles of pipe, shipped by rail and rig, stored in environmentally stable storage facilities, pumped through state-of-the-art machinery that will take a credit card AND is conveniently covered by an awning! But ink?! You just squeeze it from a plant or seed (or even chemically synthesize it in a lab), ship it via any postal carrier, and store it in a little plastic box. It doesn't even come with an awning! And what does printer ink cost? It's about $38.00 for a tablespoon! Okay, two tablespoons.

I lifted the tiny cup of juice from the silver tray as a fellow parishioner served me. I listened as the minister lifted his cup and said, "The blood of Christ, the cup of salvation." And all of a sudden, gasoline and ink seemed extremely cheap.

JD

What is your favorite Communion memory?

Spotting God...

On a Box
Behind the Pulpit

"Kids are just fearless," she said, shaking her head at our team of fifth-graders who had led us through worship on children's Sabbath. I knew what my friend was getting at, that it takes a lot of gumption to get up in front of a sanctuary full of people, LET ALONE AT TEN YEARS OLD, but I had to disagree. "Oh no, they're not fearless. Most of them were scared to death."

I had seen it at rehearsal the day before. Even though it happened every year, I crossed my fingers and prayed a prayer inside my head that we would get through this, that no one would faint or throw up on the platform. I knew we'd be fine—I really did—but I still prayed the prayer.

We gathered Saturday morning, reading and praying to empty pews, and I preached my standard sermon to the kids that our sanctuary is full of people who love them like crazy, that God loves them like crazy, and that they were doing what Pastor Jim always says we do, "making sacred space for God to do God's work," and DO YOU KNOW HOW WONDER-FUL THAT IS? DO YOU? I told them they were basically floating in a love bath; they're up near the faucet, where God turns it on; they're getting soaked in God's love even though they can't see it because it's invisible, but trust me, it's all over you. Then I decided it was time to stop gushing and reminded them to SLOW DOWN when they speak—to talk like a sloth up a tree in Madagascar would speak if it could speak English, because we all speed up when we're nervous. Speak unreasonably loud, I added, as if you're talking to your great-grandmother who left her hearing aids on her night-stand, because she just might have, and the folks working sound can only raise your volume so much. That's when I noticed that one of my cheeriest, happiest children was turning green and biting her fingernails as if they were an ear of corn.

When it was her turn to offer her prayer, one she had written herself and shown to me and was so lovely and true that it made goosebumps rise all over my body and made me utter another thank-you prayer to God that

I get to witness bare beauty like this, she stood behind the pulpit, mute. "Whenever you're ready," I said in my calmest, most comforting voice possible. "We have plenty of time."

Still nothing. Nothing.

Then tears.

"Oh! It's okay," I said as I hugged her.

Her friends joined me. "It's okay! We're all scared! You can do it!"

We gave her a moment to collect herself and let someone else practice, and then I asked her if she was ready to try again. "We'll stand with you," said a friend (these kids just kill me sometimes). So we stood with her, and she read it beautifully, and everyone cheered when she was done, including God. I could feel it!

As I sat in my chair behind the pulpit during worship on Sunday, I prayed the whole time as her prayer got nearer. Finally, it was her turn. She walked to the pulpit in small, slow steps. I prayed harder and got ready to rise and stand next to her if she needed me. I noticed her friends watching, cheering her on inside their heads. Were they praying too?

She stood a moment. Silence.

Then she prayed her beautiful prayer to the hundreds of adults in a slow, loud voice. I couldn't resist. I opened my eyes to watch her standing there on a wooden box behind the pulpit so that she could reach the microphone, leading us all to God's feet. It was breathtaking.

Fearless? No. They stand in the fear and refuse to let it win. And God and their friends stand with them. I'm so lucky I get a front-row seat to watch.

BR

When was the last time you stood in fear and refused to let it win? Did you feel God standing with you?

Spotting God...

In an Epic Fail

I HATE being weak. So I guess that explains why I was sprawled out on the bathroom floor at the doctor's office, knees under me, head down, both arms extended in front of me, as if worshiping the toilet bowl.

As I knelt there doing my square breathing, I was wishing I was a normal mommy, one who doesn't feel faint when her child gets five shots in a row in the thin skin of the underside of his forearm after an allergy panel showed no reason why his asthma had taken a dangerous turn. Why couldn't I be a mommy who didn't run away to the bathroom where she could faint in peace?

Did I lock the door? What if none of this works—the kneeling and breathing and the cold paper towel on the back of my neck? What if the nurse finishes and I'm in here unconscious, my tongue hanging out and my skirt tangled up around my waist? I'd told her I was going to get water, which was true; I'd had a sip. But then the hall started looking a little tunnel-ish, and I walked my feet in front of me, hoping I could make it around the corner before I crumpled to the floor. At least the bathroom floor was fairly clean.

It wasn't the first time I'd had an epic mommy fail. I've had to stop and put my head between my knees in doctor's offices and hospitals all across the Carolinas: when Sarah had her pre-op for her wisdom teeth removal, when Todd had his knee surgery, even during a mammogram once. But I'd never hidden myself away until now. It wasn't going very well.

And then I remembered the muffin. Months earlier, I had met my friends for coffee, and as we laughed, a crumb took a wrong turn. I started to choke a little, then held up my hand as if to say, "Don't worry; I've got control of this." I coughed and coughed, a lot at first and then just a little. But the muffin bit wouldn't quit bouncing around my windpipe. The coughing wouldn't stop. This was embarrassing. I had the urge to leave, to go outside and hack out the muffin, so I did. I ran out the door and hacked myself silly, like a cat with a hairball. Not pretty. Finally, it stopped, at the exact moment Susie opened the door.

"I was about to come help you whether you wanted it or not," she said. "You know that's what people do before they choke to death, don't you? They run off like an animal, burrowing away to die. They don't want everybody looking at them, so they go away and choke to death. It's a real thing, Becky. It's in studies."

How I love my friends.

Now, on the floor, I wondered if maybe this was a clue to my real problem. I always want to say "Don't worry; I've got control of this," but I didn't have control of this. I don't have control of much of anything, really, and neither does any of us. I can fight my fears with all my energy and end up on the floor of a toilet stall or halfway hanging from a mammogram machine. Or I can admit to the world and my friends and my God that I've got a muffin in my windpipe or I've got a child I'm terrified for or a friend with breast cancer that I'm worried about, so worried that even the sight of a mammogram machine makes me dizzy.

After I confess the truth, I can pray and let God and the people I love take care of me. I don't have to be Super Mom, able to leap tall buildings or stay standing when I'm scared. I can just be Squeamish Human Mom, sometimes terribly strong and sometimes embarrassingly weak. That's enough for God. It needs to be enough for me.

BR

When was your last epic fail? What did God teach you through it? What are you still learning or working on?

Spotting God...

In Autumn's Release

I cranked my harvest-moon-colored VW Beetle, put the top down, buttoned my jacket (it was 41 degrees outside), and drove a familiar route to the First Baptist Church, Greenville, this morning. From East Park Avenue, I turned left on Main, left on Academy, right on McBee, and left onto McDaniel.

Ahhhh, McDaniel. Some mornings I take other paths to arrive at 847 Cleveland Street. But in autumn I love driving down McDaniel. The woven limbs of an array of hardwoods provide a spectacular canopy overhead. And during the autumn season the ceiling of the Sistine Chapel couldn't rival this natural, artistic blend of texture, light, and color.

As I rolled beneath these holy arches, a gust of wind shook the boughs above. I laughed to myself as hundreds of little leaves fell and floated and scattered in the seat and floorboards around me. It was as if God had thrown a ticker-tape parade just for me! I wondered what I had done to deserve such a display of heavenly affection and accolade? Was Sunday's sermon really that good? Was it the one extra visit I made this week? Was God pleased that I was trying to do my best to live this life with some integrity? None of these deeds seemed to warrant a heavenly ticker-tape parade. In fact, nothing good I could ever do or ever imagine doing would warrant the kind of affection God has lavished on me—from the tress on McDaniel or Calvary's tree. I just watched the leaves fall, smiled, and breathed a soft "Thank you, God."

I stopped spiritually "beating myself up" a long time ago. It finally sank in—after years of tears and confessions and promises and re-promises and worries and various other forms of mental/spiritual flagellation—that God loves me. I did nothing to deserve it; I can do nothing to maintain it or lose it. The wind blows where it wills. The leaves fall upon me because of the intentional, mysterious, graceful love of God. If God loves me that way, then God also loves you that way.

So if you're driving up McDaniel and the wind of God blows and the leaves fall on you, slow down. Enjoy the parade. It's in your honor. You are a beloved child of God. Look toward heaven and breathe a soft "Thank you, God."

JD

In what simple ways might God be lavishing love upon you?

Spotting God...

In Tardiness

My alarm goes off at 5:00 a.m. every morning. Yep, even Saturdays and Sundays. In the ensuing minutes the dog is walked, a cup of coffee is consumed, the newspaper is perused, and I'm out the door before 6:00 to swim, bike, or run. It's the life of an aspiring triathlete.

This morning, I didn't get up until 5:30. I had scheduled a run today, but by the time all necessary routines were accomplished, it was 6:15. I just didn't want to run at 6:15. I wouldn't get to nod, wave, and speak to my usual fellow athletes. I'd have to commune with those lazy heathen who get up later. Needing the miles and meditation, however (and feeling a bit of a "holy nudge"), I exited the house and hit the road.

I ran up Craddock Way, took a left on Rivoli Drive, another left on Northside Drive, and settled into a nice pace. Northside Drive. We have a friend who lives off Northside Drive—Pam. Her father died tragically just two days ago; his funeral is today. I whispered a prayer for her.

I rounded the curve just before the fire station, looked up, and saw Pam walking toward me. Tears were streaming down her face. Her eyes were puffy with grief. She looked relieved to see me. She walked right into my sweaty arms, and we stood by the road holding each other. After a long and lovely moment of silence, I finally whispered in her ear, "You are in my prayers today. Keep walking." She released the embrace, stepped back, patted her heart (because she could not talk), and we moved on.

JD

When have you crossed paths with God by crossing paths
with another cherished human being?

Spotting God...

While Sharing
an Armrest

Ani DiFranco rocks the Variety Playhouse in Atlanta's Little Five Points at least once a year. This year, I had to officiate a wedding on the evening of the concert—70 miles away, at 6:00 p.m. I hooked them quick, then hoofed it to ATL; I made it with time to spare. I wouldn't miss Ani. She's a modern-day prophet.

Yeah, yeah, I know. She's a lesbian (or at least bisexual). She had a child out of wedlock last year, and she weaves the "F word" into the lyrics of some of her songs. But give her a break. Isaiah is the leadoff pitcher of the canonized Major Prophets, and he walked around naked in Egypt for several years! (What's that confused look on your face? Read your Bible; it's in there.)

I subtly surveyed the audience as they gathered. The crowd was a cabaret in and of itself. It took only a moment to notice I was the only white, straight, middle-aged, Baptist male in attendance (in fact, choose any two of those adjectives, and I was probably still the lone representative). But I was welcomed, barely noticed.

Before the first sounds were flung from Ani's signature Alvarez Yairi ADY1 acoustic guitar (music-loving guy thing), Roxy and I negotiated the armrest that separated us and shared a little conversation. Roxy is my concert-going, coffee-shop-chatting, lesbian friend. We small-talked about our favorite Ani tunes. Then I scanned the gathered groupies and wondered aloud, "Does the church have anything to offer this crowd?" Roxy quickly turned to me and responded, "The church has plenty to offer this crowd, but you won't let us in!" I started to once again defend my weekly worshipers, but her pierced nose and piercing eyes demanded I keep the conversation honest. I know what I know, but I know what she meant.

We sat and sang and smiled together as Ani called us to worship, prayed a poem, sang her familiar hymns, provoked us with poignant phrases and a cutting laugh. She challenged us to make the world a better place and then sent us on our way. Yep, Ani is a prophet—one Righteous Babe (the name of her record label).

JD

In what strange places have you been welcomed into the presence of God?

Spotting God...

In a
Needle and Thread

"Does God ever change his mind?" a child asked me.

"I'm wondering what you think about that," I said. "And what is making you ask that good question."

"Well, I've been reading these Bible stories—by myself, you know—and DO PEOPLE KNOW WHAT'S IN THERE? There's a lot of bad stuff!" he said. "Like plagues and even babies killed—or about to be killed—and babies didn't do anything. It doesn't seem like God would do that. I asked my mom, and she said that God is the same yesterday, today, and tomorrow. But I just wonder about that."

Such big questions.

So I told him a story, one of my favorites. God created the world and put Adam and Eve in the garden of Eden. They could eat from any tree in the garden except for the tree of good and evil. *"Eat from that tree,"* God said, *"and you will die."* So what happened? They ate from the tree, saw they were naked, made clothes out of fig leaves, and hid from God. And what did God do? Did God follow through on his word? Did God put them to death? No. God went after them and told them their consequences (which were tough and not fun), and God noticed them in their flimsy fig-clothes (which didn't even fit). And what did God do? HE SEWED THEM CLOTHES HIMSELF.

God had promised death but delivered mercy. It happens over and over in that big, confusing, wonderful book. God changes God's mind, offering mercy to broken, mixed-up people.

Plus, there's Jesus, who gives us a clearer picture of who God is—Jesus, whose favorite things to do are to love God, love people, and offer them mercy. It's Jesus Christ who is the same yesterday and today and forever

(Heb 13:8). Yay for that. When we are in doubt of who God is at the heart, we can always look to Jesus.

Yes, God changes his mind, always offering mercy. May we be ready to do the same.

BR

For whom might you need to pick up a needle and thread and sew some mercy?

Spotting God...

In a Lincoln Log House

One thing I love most about children (or maybe I should say "other people's children") is that they don't mind saying out loud what they're thinking deep inside—at least, until we teach them to filter themselves, to hide thoughts that might embarrass themselves or us.

Today, I'm thinking about a particular unfiltered comment from a child a few years ago. A Sunday school teacher had just shared with our second-graders the sacred story about the people who brought their paralyzed friend to see Jesus. Since the house where he was teaching was too crowded, they took their friend up to the roof, peeled back some tiles, and lowered him down in front of Jesus, who healed him.

After the story the teacher asked, "*Which part of the story did you like best?*"

Everyone's hand went up. The children loved the Lincoln Log house we use to tell the story; they loved removing the roof and looking inside; they loved the stretcher with the man on it; they loved that Jesus healed him; they loved that the friends wouldn't let a roof or a crowd stand in the way of their friend's need to walk. And did I mention that they really, really loved the Lincoln Log house?

Then the teacher moved to the next question: "*I wonder how the paralyzed man felt when his friends told him they would take him to see Jesus.*"

What would you expect them to say?

Excited, because he wants to walk!

Happy he has friends who care!

Wondering how they will get through the crowds.

Happy he will meet Jesus, who will fix his legs.

But one child had a different perspective. I still remember the child's honest response to the story. I saved it in my heart as a treasure, even though it was a little painful to hear: "*I'd be afraid,*" the child said. "*What if they go* to all that trouble and it doesn't work? What if Jesus can heal everybody else but it doesn't work with me?"

Oh, child. I've felt that too. Have you ever wondered if you bring some secret ugliness or shame or otherness that is beyond fixing or saving or loving?

Bless this child for voicing it so we can talk about it. We can share the message that NO ONE can bring anything or dream up anything or be anything God cannot love or heal. No one.

You are loved, child, exactly as you are! Don't be afraid! It's the truth. I'm so thankful I have children around to remind me of that.

BR

What secret shame or ugliness or otherness could you bring bravely to God's loving light?

Spotting God...

In a Homeless Grandmother

Her name was Gertrude, and she told me she was 74 years old. "I never imagined I would be living like this," she said, looking around at the Sunday school room our church had made into a bedroom for a homeless family for the week. "Homeless? At my age? Why, I've always had a home." She ran a hand through her thinning hair and then rested it on the growth on her neck. The growth worried me. I tried not to stare. "But I had to take Maggie out of that house," she said, looking away. "I worked all my life in a doctor's office. But here I am."

We walked to the game room and sat down on plastic chairs to watch her granddaughter play air hockey with the other children. She was a tiny little girl with a face like a moon, big blue eyes and a mane of curly hair neatly clipped with a barrette. Her nose was stuffed up, so she kept her mouth open to breathe as she played.

"Maggie, come here," Gertrude said as she held up a tissue. "Blow. There, that's good." She fished lip balm out of her pants pocket. "Stay still." Gertrude smeared it on her lips and nodded for Maggie to go back to playing.

Gertrude looked at the other children. "Those little girls there, they've been so good to her. Lord knows Maggie needs them. She gets lonesome with it being just me and her. It's been nearly a year now since her momma left, and she still cries for her, at night especially. And her momma hasn't one time called or come to see her, not once. I thought she might on Maggie's birthday, but she didn't. At the school she goes to, the mommas, they come in to help in the classroom. I said to her, I said, 'Maggie, I could come in and help your teacher,' but she said she didn't want me to."

Gertrude raised her head, looked at me, and her eyes began to glisten. "I asked her if she was—if she was ashamed of me," she said. "She said no. She said that all the other kids have their mommas. She didn't want them to know that she didn't have no momma. I think it's the word *momma* that means so much to her. It's the word that means so much."

"But it's so wonderful that Maggie has you."

"Well, I do the best I can for her, but I'm not her momma. But I guess it's just as well her momma's gone with her drinking like she does. She's Spanish, so I put her over at this school where they teach the children Spanish so maybe one day she could talk with her. But I don't know if it's ever going to happen. I'm not going to let her momma do anything to hurt her, that's for sure. And her daddy, my son, he was living with us, but I'm sorry to say that he's just as bad or worse. And one night it got so bad that I just packed us up and we left with little more than the clothes on our backs. So here we are."

"You're taking such good care of her."

"Oh, I'll take care of her. I'll take care of her if it's the last thing I do. But she does have some nice friends at school, so it's not so bad. Her best little friend at school is Dr. Morgan's little girl. Do you know Dr. Morgan? He's a good man, a nice family. They had us stay with them over Christmas, and they made it so nice for us. They even bought us presents. I wish I could have given them something, but I guess they understood. They did let me fix some cornbread for them to have at Christmas dinner. Dr. Morgan says you just can't find good cornbread around here, and he sat there and ate three pieces. Three! I tell you, it did my heart good to see him enjoy it so. It was a gift to me, that's what it was."

As I wait to celebrate the arrival of the Christ child to our hurting world, I'm thinking I've already seen him. He was sitting in a plastic chair, lip balm in one hand, tissue in the other.

BR

Have you seen the face of Christ already this season?
What did he look like?

Spotting God...

In a
Candy Cane Riot

Our caroling trip to the retirement center was going great! Not only had we not lost any of our 29 children, but they were doing an amazing job following our *"Rules for Visiting a Retirement Center/Nursing Home,"* which I'd had them make before we boarded the bus. I like to phrase things in a positive manner, but these kids tend to lay down the law plain and simple. The rules were as follows: Don't eat their food. Don't touch their stuff. Don't say rude things. Mind your manners, and sing loudly, but not so loudly as to be annoying.

The ladies at our first stop were practically salivating over how adorable the children were, and I had to agree. The women tilted their heads adoringly during *"Away in a Manger"* and bounced their heads along to *"Rudolph the Red-nosed Reindeer,"* clasping their hands in glee when Martin added "like George Washington!"

After a rousing rendition of *"We Wish You a Merry Christmas,"* it was time to move to our next stop. But then I remembered the candy canes! I hadn't told the children we'd be handing out candy canes. No problem. I'd do it now.

"Thank you for letting us sing to you," I said to our smitten audience. "We have some treats we'd like to hand out to you. Children, if you'd like to help give each of these friends a candy cane, I have plenty in my bag."

Before I even got the word *bag* out of my mouth, 58 arms rooted into the plastic grocery bag, nearly tugging it out of my hands. Candy canes flew through the air and snapped on the floor. These people were on a mission! Girls and boys strode across the room with an important job to do. Strangers needed candy, and God had brought us to deliver! Even our most shy children wanted in on the action. They quickly returned to my bag, big grins on their faces: "Can I have another?" A few children returned frustrated: "Everybody has one already!" Not to worry, I told them. We'd have plenty more stops to make.

"That was GREAT!" said one of my third-grade girls as we walked through the corridors to our next stop.

"Yes, they loved your singing," I said.

"No, Miss Becky, not that. It's the candy canes! I LOVED giving out the candy canes! I could do that thing all day!"

It was interesting. Each child loved giving out candy canes. Every single one. They could hardly wait to put their hands on them, touch them (not pocket them), and pass them along to someone who might need one.

It was as if the task were holy. I've decided it was.

Maybe that's why this Santa thing has caught on so well. We do something simple like trying on a red suit or handing out candy canes, and before we know it, we taste what it's like to be the Greatest Giver of All!

BR

What was the best time you've ever had giving a gift?
What would you say is the best gift in your life that God
has given to you?

Spotting God...

Within the
Christmas Invasion

I try my best to avoid the mall around Christmas. When I find myself herded with strangers between purse displays under signs that say *Believe*, I have the urge to make mooing noises and yell, "No, I don't *BELIEVE* in shopping, and I'll be leaving this hell on earth right now, thank you, to go to a neighborhood shop where I won't be pulled into the undertow and end up buying tube socks for everybody just to get the presents checked off my list!"

I'm a Christmas lover for sure, but I recognize that it's an invasion into the quasi-sanity of our normal lives. Christmas has a way of taking over, don't you think? It invades our living rooms, our schedules, our bank accounts, and our radio stations. Sometimes it's good, sometimes it's heavenly, and sometimes it just hands out headaches like the sample lady at Costco.

So how do we keep our focus on an "invasion of holiness," as Frederick Buechner describes Christmas—the kind that charges us with electric hope rather than the commercial version, which drains and exhausts us and makes us seek comfort in fudge and eggnog? How do we shepherd our thoughts away from the nagging worries and fearful panic of this world, toward the God who "invaded" our world in baby skin and then watched and waited to see how it all would unfold? Toward the God who breathed his holiness over the manger scene as Mary groaned and animals stirred? Toward the God who breathes over us still as we groan and stir and love each other, as we do life heroically and terribly and everything in between? How do keep our eyes on the holy and divine while the world goes on with its craziness? Really? How do we do it at the mall?

I asked some children for advice on this; as usual, they had wise things to say:

1. Try a lot of times to look at the top of the tree. Now, you'll most likely find an angel there or a star, and either is good because an angel is just a messenger of God, sent to you to bring you peace, and the star is the

thing that showed people where to find Jesus. So it's going to point you to peace or to Jesus. You're in good shape either way.

2. Tell the Christmas story over and over inside your head. Not the Santa and the elves one, no. The Jesus and the shepherds and Mary and Joseph one. Concentrate on the "do not be afraid" and the "tidings of great joy" parts. Those are two good things to think about.

3. Don't get too much on your brain about Christmas presents. I know it's hard, but if the present breaks, you're done with. It's over. If you spend your time thinking of God, that can't break. At least you'll have that, and it doesn't get old.

4. Stop running around, and sit down for five minutes and just think. You can have coffee if you want. That's what my mom does.

5. Pray. You can do that inside your head, and no one will even know.

6. Look up at the sky and remember that someone's up there watching us and caring about us. That should help.

7. Think about the angels singing. If you can't hear it, then sing yourself. You can be like an angel and tell yourself the good news.

I told you, wise girls and wise boys, these kids!

BR

Have you felt an invasion of holiness this season or an invasion of a less spiritual kind? What do you plan to do to keep your eyes on the holy and divine?

Spotting God...

In Third Grade

Because I am considered a "progressive" member of the clergy, I'm often asked to speak at public schools during holiday seasons. A few years ago during the "winter holiday season" (school-talk for Christmas), I was asked to share with a group of third-graders the meanings of Christmas, Chanukah, and Kwanzaa.

While awaiting my introduction and allotted block of time, I eavesdropped on the preliminary conversation between students. A young Jewish boy (the legitimate reason for school-talk during Christmas) was explaining to a Christian classmate the historical origin of Chanukah. For a third-grader, he did a splendid and thorough job of conveying the facts of this miraculous story. His eyes were wide with enthusiasm as he expounded upon the intricacies of the Romans, the Maccabees, and the temple menorah.

Upon finishing his story, the gentile guy aggressively responded, "My dad told me there's no way a little bit of oil could have burned eight nights! Christmas is the only real holiday!"

On cue, the kosher kid calmly replied, "Well, my dad told me virgins can't have babies!"

Their vocal volumes escalated, and the teacher attempted a quick intervention, but not before some little girl asked what oil and virgins have to do with each other.

I can tolerate almost anything but intolerance. When it comes right down to it, the things we believe are precious simply because we believe them. They are downright silly to those who don't believe. We need to be okay with that. My silliness doesn't have to trump your silliness. My truth doesn't have to trump your truth. God has the power and right to reveal divine presence any way God chooses. God understands the connection between oil and virgins.

JD

*What elements of faiths other than your own have
informed your own sense of God's power and presence?*

Spotting God...

In the Crowd

We stood in line for over an hour and finally reached the top. The roof was packed with camera-toting, awe-inspired, loud people. Did I say packed?

I like the quiet. I have no problem being alone; in fact, I tend to seek out sanctuaries of solace. I've always resonated with Elijah's mountain moment—a place where wind and fire and earthquake could not conjure what the quiet would provide. While I love the art of preaching and often feed on the well-crafted sermons of colleagues, I am typically more drawn to meditation rather than the mental meanderings of a fellow human being. I know everyone isn't bent this way; I am.

My bend has often lured me into less-than-perfect situations. Several years ago, for instance, I led a mission team to New York City's post-9/11 environment. We spent several days working with a local congregation— building a new playground, teaching children, and repairing a building. Every minute of the mission experience was carefully crafted on my meticulously timed itinerary. Copies of such were distributed to all participants, and if I may say so, I had done a fabulous job of ensuring that our team would have an experience they would remember for a lifetime.

Our first evening in the Big Apple was to be spent in prayer. Before laying a hand on a hammer or sharing a word with a city citizen, I wanted us to pray. What better place than the top of the Empire State Building— our group standing there, looking out over the electrically lit city, holding hands in the quiet, all alone, praying? After all, I'd seen the 1993 cinematic tearjerker *Sleepless in Seattle*. I watched as Tom Hanks and Meg Ryan held hands and gazed lovingly at each other. Our group would have the top of the Empire State Building *all to ourselves*.

We stood in line for over an hour and finally reached the top. The roof was packed with camera-toting, awe-inspired, loud people. Did I say packed? (A month ago I was in Las Vegas. I went to watch the Bellagio fountains. I'm such a savvy traveler now. I knew there would be a crowd, and I knew no one from the *Ocean's Eleven* cast would be standing there. Live and learn.)

We joined the crowd, and we got loud, and I think we all prayed—rubbing shoulders with the world and gazing through our camera lenses at the skyline of the city. And God was there.

Sometimes I like it when God gets noisy.

JD

It's often easy to sense God's presence in the quiet of a lonely place. When have you felt God's presence in a bustling crowd?

Spotting God...

In the Fast Lane

Riverside Drive is a four-lane access road that runs parallel to Interstate 75 on the eastern edge of the mini-metropolis of Macon, Georgia. According to the Department of Transportation, it is one of the three busiest traffic arteries in our fair city. Last week, I was headed south on Riverside Drive toward the Macon City Auditorium. I, along with a carload of concert companions, was en route to see what was left of Gordon Lightfoot. As we topped the hill where Riverside Drive intersects Wimbish Road, we slammed on brakes. Someone was changing a flat tire. The rear end of the pimped-out El Camino was lifted by a jack. The tattered tire had been removed and was lying beside the bare axle. The driver was hoisting the spare tire toward the car and would in moments tighten the lug nuts.

So what's wrong with this picture? Our driver in distress was fixing his flat in the fast lane of Riverside Drive! There were numerous driveways to numerous parking lots along this busy thoroughfare, but he had stopped in the middle of the fast lane to change his tire! Traffic was stopping, staggering, staring, and struggling to safely veer around him. His personal crisis became a crisis for everyone who came in contact with him.

I've endured a few crises in the course of my short life. In the fast lane of family and ministry and social engagement, I've had to stop and fix a few tattered moments and relationships. At the time these crises seemed to be the very center of my existence—dominating my energy, thoughts, and actions. Now, however, I'm wondering how often I made them the center of everyone else's existence. Did I "pull over" for repairs to await the assistance of some good Samaritan or friend? Or did I just stop in front of God and everybody, expecting them to adjust their agendas to my anguish?

No one in our car cursed or criticized the needy traveler. And there was no way we could stop and help. Like everyone else in every other car, we just swerved and laughed at a man so self- consumed with crisis that he was oblivious to the harmful and helpful realities around him.

JD

***What crises have you endured, and how do you imagine
you have allowed them to affect others?***

105

Spotting God...
While Coasting

I'm following Don Fink's training plan toward my first Ironman distance triathlon. In his book titled *Be Iron Fit*, he provides three 30-week workout schedules: a competitive schedule (time-consuming and tough), a "just finish" schedule (relatively easy for the amateur athlete), and an intermediate schedule (somewhere in between the other two). I'm committed to the intermediate schedule, and I've only got 20 weeks to go. The Vineman Ironman—in Napa Valley, California—is held on July 29, 2012. I'm registered. I'm going to be an Ironman...

I'm contemplating adjusting Don Fink's schedule. Last Saturday, I was scheduled to ride my bike for 2 hours and 45 minutes. I happened to be out of town—away from my bike. The weather was threatening; I couldn't ride outside. Fortunately, a local fitness center allowed me to make use of one of their stationary bicycles for the allotted time. Two hours into the ride I had a thought (always a dangerous moment for me): *I'm riding at a steady pace. I'm constantly spinning the pedals, but if the race is partially* uphill, *then it must be partially* downhill, *so I need to add a little coasting into my training!* Having pedaled for two hours, I assumed it would be fine to skip the last 45 minutes of the ride and log that in my journal as "coasting time." I wondered what Don Fink would think of my alteration to his training schedule—and then I kept pedaling for the final 45 minutes...

I'm celebrating Sabbath today. I'm glad God stopped pedaling for a while and gave me permission—gave me a command—to do the same.

JD

When was the last time you did nothing for a day?
What was that like, or what might that be like?

Spotting God...
In a Cat on a String

Several years ago around this time, my daughter called her daddy from college about the Christmas gift he planned to give me. "Dad, I'm telling you, it's a bad idea," she said. "Mom said after Katie died that she doesn't want another cat."

"She wants one," he said. "Trust me. I know her."

I didn't want another cat. Katie the cat had been our baby when Todd and I were newlyweds, when we acted like fools in love, throwing her birthday parties and taking her with us on weekend trips from Washington, DC, to her "grandparents'" house in North Carolina. During one trip to Fayetteville, she curled up behind Todd's neck while he was driving and peed down his shirt. Maybe it was payback for the days ahead. She endured life with three rambunctious children, plus a move to France and back. She was a great indoor cat, and I loved her, but after eighteen years of scooping the litter box, I was done.

Besides, I thought I had been pretty generous to entertain a cat so long, considering my upbringing. When I once worried to my mom, the most loving woman I know, about the neighbor's cat who was stuck up a tree in our front yard, Mom said, "Honey, go do your homework. I've never seen a cat skeleton in a tree."

I didn't need a cat. We already had Tanner the Slobber Dog, who was more than enough animal to handle. Despite his hours of obedience classes, he was not obedient—sweet as sugar, but more than enough pet for a family of five.

Even if I wanted a second animal, the timing wasn't right. That Christmas season was one of the hardest times of my family's life. One of our children was very, very sick. We were living day-to-day, exhausted and worried and hanging on by a thread. Our world had tightened into a small little sphere, a bubble of our own, enclosing our house, enlarging only for drives back and forth from the doctor's office. No matter. Todd carried into the house a black cat with a red bow on its head, and Christmas officially came early. "I knew you'd love her!" he said and handed her off to me.

Sarah followed me around the kitchen, asking, "Are you sure you're okay with this?" I was. Libby was cute, and it was fun to focus on something besides our own fears.

Libby let Tanner know who was in charge right away. Now we just had to turn Libby into an indoor/outdoor cat since I was determined not to deal with a litter box forever. But how would this work? Our yard backed up to a very busy road. A cat could become a pancake in a second.

We kept her inside a few weeks, just to make sure she knew this was home, but then the time finally came. I tied the end of a ball of yarn to her collar and took her outside. Little by little, I let out the yarn, and little by little, she stopped acting like the sky might fall down on her like a big blue blanket. She would go as far as the fence and then come back. I would watch and talk to her, reeling the yarn in and out.

We kept at it over several days. Every time, it felt familiar to me, and then I realized why. Holding a string on our cat mirrored just what we were doing with our sick child (and with our other kids, really) all their lives. Birthing them into a nice safe bubble, then letting them out, little by little, pulling them back sometimes, and other times letting the string go really slack. Finally, we had to untie the strings and hope for the best. We had to let go, or they couldn't be what they were meant to be. They couldn't be part of the BIG LIFE God had for them under that blue blanket of sky.

Maybe the string felt familiar too because I recognized the tugging of an even greater invisible string hanging from my own heart—the one gently drawing me (and you too?) toward a God who loves me. "I led them with cords of human kindness," says Hosea 11:4, "with ties of love. To them I was like one who lifts a little child to the cheek, and I bent down to feed them." God pulls us toward him through the love and kindnesses of other humans we encounter. I love it! God stands in the yard with the string of our kindnesses to each other, saying, "Becky, Becky, come to me; come to me."

It quiets my mother's heart to know that no matter what happens once I put the yarn down, God stays out there in the yard, calling my children and yours, me and you, all of us, to God's cheek, to let God feed us and love us more deeply that we can understand.

So what happened with Libby and her string? We finally untied her, set her free to begin her BIG LIFE. She did. And our children did too. Our sick child became well; all three kept growing into the people God created them to be. They all had moments of thriving (and sometimes just surviving, including Libby).

As for Libby, that cat was climbing trees before we knew it—and occasionally getting stuck. But don't worry; Mom was right. No cat skeleton sightings in our tree—not yet anyway.

BR

What or who has been on the end of your string?
Is it time to ask God to help you let go?

Spotting God...

On the Calendar

As a minister, theologian, and general lover of all things spiritual, I spend a great portion of my time either promoting or dispelling mystery. Oddly enough, our post-enlightenment, overly scientific generation has a strange tendency to embrace mystery where there is none. We so crave something beyond our rational knowledge that we make up "mystery" to keep our minds and hearts intrigued.

Recently, a young professional—wide-eyed with wonder—told me his maternal grandmother and one of his paternal aunts both died on the same date, and add to that, his son shares a birthdate with one of his cousins! He concluded his utterings of amazement by excitedly asking, "Can you believe that?" I paused. I always hate it when I have to dispel a cherished "mystery." But I did my job. I informed my friend that, statistically, if you gather 25 people in a room, quite likely two of them share a birthdate. This is truly no mystery. There are over seven billion people on the face of our planet and only 365 days in the year on which to be born, get married, die, and experience all other life events. There's going to be a lot of crossover.

On the other hand, promoting mystery is no easier. We often struggle to embrace real mystery—such as the mystery of God's presence, grace, and love. We regularly read from a book that is thousands of years old. We pray to a God we cannot see and say God is with us. We gather in a space that has been sanctuary for thousands, lift bread and wine to our mouths, and watch young people submerged in holy waters. Some Sundays it moves us. Other Sundays we wonder what we're doing here, what we'll cook for lunch, and did I close the garage door.

It's easy for us to believe there is some enigmatic significance to a shared birthdate but hard for us to believe God is with us, God loves us, and God is infinitely merciful to us. It's even harder to believe these things are true for others. It's often easier to share a birthdate than it is to share grace.

JD

What calendar dates are special to you, and why? (Enjoy them, and don't let my analytical cynicism convince you to do otherwise.)

Terrific, you're still here!

Either you decided to stick with us through all our dumpster-diving for God in the messiness of our lives, or you're a back-to-front reader and you just haven't given us the chance to perplex or offend you yet! Either way, we hope you'll forgive us our trespasses. We're only plodding through life like you, groping in the darkness for a God who calls our names. We figure that if we really believe that we live and move through life in God, why not track down traces of holiness along the way? So we're keeping our eyes open, talking to witnesses, dusting for fingerprints, and searching for clues. It's holy detective work. No surprise that we both like murder mysteries (okay, so Jim goes for horror flicks like *Saw* while Becky likes Agatha Christie's *Poirot*—all that blood from *Saw* would send her to the floor!)!

Even if our journaling feels odd to you or our interpretations differ-ent, we hope you'll join us in our semi-sacred game of I Spy. You can start right where you are. Really, put down your coffee cup; pick up your messy, unironed yesterday from the corner where you dropped it before you sank into bed (no judgment here!); rifle through its pockets; and give it a gentle, loving shake for the divine. You might be surprised how often something holy falls out.

Or take the game with you as you head into tomorrow. You never know; God might reveal himself in a sunny thunderstorm or blindside you in the middle of your toddler's tantrum. You just might stand there and hear yourself ask, "What's a nice God like you doing in a place like this?" It's okay. God surely wouldn't mind our perfect pickup line, given that he spends our lives wooing us back home where we belong.

Blessings on your journey,

Becky and Jim

CPSIA information can be obtained
at www.ICGtesting.com
Printed in the USA
FFOW05n1848261016

9 780989 575331